ISLAMOPHOBIA

RELIGIOUS INTOLERANCE AGAINST MUSLIMS TODAY

PUBLIC PERSECUTIONS   Alison Morretta

Cavendish
Square

New York

Published in 2017 by Cavendish Square Publishing, LLC
243 5th Avenue, Suite 136, New York, NY 10016

Copyright © 2017 by Cavendish Square Publishing, LLC

First Edition

Library of Congress Cataloging-in-Publication Data

Names: Morretta, Alison.
Title: Islamaphobia: religious intolerance against Muslims today / Alison Morretta.
Description: New York : Cavendish Square Publishing, 2017.
| Series: Public persecutions | Includes index.
Identifiers: ISBN 9781502623317 (library bound) | ISBN 9781502623324 (ebook)
Subjects: LCSH: Islamophobia. | Islam–Public opinion. | War on Terrorism, 2001-2009.
Classification: LCC BP52.M67 2017 | DDC 305.6'97–dc23

Editorial Director: David McNamara
Editor: Fletcher Doyle
Copy Editor: Nathan Heidelberger
Associate Art Director: Amy Greenan
Designer: Jessica Nevins
Production Coordinator: Karol Szymczuk
Photo Research: J8 Media

Contents

Roots of Discrimination

The founding principles of the United States of America provide its citizens with inalienable rights and freedoms. Among these rights are freedom of religion, freedom of speech, freedom of assembly, protection from unlawful search or seizure, and the right to a speedy and public trial. The Declaration of Independence boldly declares, "We hold these truths to be self-evident, that all men are created equal," but over the course of American history, there have been many times when these principles and laws have been ignored. Often in times of crisis, out of fear, people start to believe that it is acceptable to compromise the liberties of others for some misguided sense of security.

The terrorist attacks on September 11, 2001, changed the face of modern America. However, the United States has a long history of discrimination against those considered to be outside the white, Protestant Christian norm. Religious persecution in particular has been a common theme since

Opposite: Worshippers examine some of the $200,000 in property damage at the unfinished Mubarak Mosque in Chantilly, Virginia, on February 17, 2012.

colonial times. Over the years, Catholics, Jews, and Muslims have been singled out for oppression. Even though it certainly existed in the twentieth century, since 9/11, the persecution of Muslims in the United States has become more common. A culture of **Islamophobia** pervades American politics, laws, and media, and it is only getting worse.

The term Islamophobia was popularized after a British **think tank** called the Runnymede Trust commissioned a report on Islamophobia in Britain. The most basic definition of the term comes from the 1997 Runnymede report: "unfounded hostility towards Muslims, and therefore fear or dislike of all or most Muslims." The definition in today's world is more complex than that, and is better defined by a Center for American Progress study, *Fear, Inc.*: "an exaggerated fear, hatred, and hostility toward Islam and Muslims that is perpetuated by negative stereotypes resulting in bias, discrimination, and the marginalization and exclusion of Muslims from America's social, political, and civil life." This second definition more accurately reflects the current US-specific culture of Islamophobia after 9/11.

There are several core beliefs that characterize Islamophobia:

- Islam is **monolithic**, static, and unable to adapt to modern life
- Islam is separate and other
- Islam is seen as inferior (i.e., barbaric, irrational, primitive, sexist)

- Islam is violent, aggressive, threatening, supportive of terrorism, engaged in "a clash of civilizations" with the West
- Islam is not a religion but a political ideology, used for political or military advantage
- Criticisms made by Islam of "the West" are not valid or correct
- Hostility toward Islam justifies discriminatory practices towards Muslims and exclusion of Muslims from mainstream society
- Anti-Muslim hostility is a normal and natural response

In post-9/11 America, these beliefs are reinforced by the news media, the entertainment industry, politicians, and religious leaders. Americans are bombarded with images, news stories, and misinformation painting all Muslims as dangerous fanatics and portraying the religion of Islam as a violent threat to the American way of life.

After 9/11, the US government enacted legislation and started the ongoing War on Terror in the Middle East. These attacks and the subsequent wars caused the first major wave of post-9/11 Islamophobia. Over the years, the Middle East has grown more unstable and terrorism is thriving, in part because Islamophobic behavior and laws actually help terrorists in their recruitment efforts. Although it never really went away, the second major wave of post-9/11 Islamophobia occurred at the end of the decade after a series of smaller-scale attacks on US soil brought the fear of homegrown terrorism to the forefront of Islamophobic discourse.

Islamophobic beliefs all too often lead to acts of violence and hate, and this affects not just American Muslims but also non-Muslim Arabs, Sikhs, and anyone else who is thought to look Muslim. Even though not all Arabs are Muslim and

Syrian Orthodox Christians participate in a Christmas procession in the city of Bethlehem, in the West Bank. The Middle East has a long history of religious diversity.

Islamophobia: Religious Intolerance Against Muslims Today

Islam is an incredibly diverse religion practiced by many different races and ethnicities, Arab Americans have been the target of most of the attacks and suspicion. They have also been disproportionately targeted by law enforcement, to the extent that ethnic and religious profiling has become standard practice in the United States.

The rise of ISIS and the 2016 presidential election campaign sparked a third major wave of Islamophobia. Republican presidential nominee Donald Trump announced that, if elected, he would ban all Muslim immigrants from entering the United States at a time when conflict in the Middle East was fueling a major refugee crisis. Such pronouncements have fanned the flames of racism and **xenophobia** in the United States.

There are 3.3 million Muslims in America (1 percent of the total US population as of 2015), and that population is expected to double by 2050. Muslims are not going away, and it is time for America to accept that they are as much a part of the fabric of America as anyone else. With both Islamophobia and the Muslim population rising, the nation's future relationship with its Muslim residents is uncertain, but the outlook certainly is not hopeless. There are many organizations, interfaith groups, and activists working hard to protect those whose lives have been affected by religious persecution and bigotry. Education, interfaith dialogue, and personal relationships are the most important tools in fighting the culture of Islamophobia in America. Americans must come together to fight for the values they hold dear so that all of the country's citizens are truly free.

ONE

A History of Violence

As of 2016, the Muslim American population was around 3.3 million, or 1 percent of the total population of the United States. This number is expected to increase in the coming years as America becomes more ethnically and religiously diverse. With the growing Muslim population, there has been growing concern, bigotry, and outright violence against the percentage of the population that identifies as Muslim. This prejudice also extends to, among others, non-Muslim Arabs, Persians, Palestinians, Assyrians, and Sikhs.

Religious persecution has a long history in America. When the Constitution was being drafted, there were debates over whether non-Protestants (which included Catholics, Muslims, and Jews) should be able to hold political office. Although these religious qualifiers did not ultimately become federal law, many state constitutions adopted this rule and imposed other restrictions on the civil liberties of religious minorities.

Opposite: **A group of first-wave Arab immigrants arrives at Ellis Island in New York, 1907. Their dress indicates they are likely Muslims from the Ottoman Empire (Turkey).**

Throughout American history—in periods often corresponding to national crises, economic downturns, and/or large waves of immigration—Americans tend to adopt an **isolationist** and **nativist** attitude. As prejudice against nonwhite, non-Christian "others" becomes more socially acceptable, discrimination, hate speech, and violence become more common. Religious persecution began with the Catholics, continued with the Jews, reared up against followers of Shinto from Japan, and is now focused on the Muslims.

First-Wave Arab Immigration

Anti-Muslim bias has existed in America since the first European settlers brought with them a historical antagonism between Christianity and Islam that stretched back to the religious wars known as the Crusades (1095–1291). The earliest Muslims in America were people brought from North and West Africa and sold into slavery in the colonies. Slaves were treated as less than human and were not allowed to practice their religion, so the Islamic faith virtually disappeared in the next generation.

The nation's first immigration law, the Naturalization Act of 1790, stated that only free white persons could become American citizens. This played an important role during the first major wave of Muslim immigration to the United States, which took place from the 1880s to the 1920s. During this time period more than twenty million people from all over the world immigrated to the United States. The first wave of Arab immigrants were from Greater Syria, which includes the present-day countries Syria, Lebanon, Jordan, Palestine, and Israel. These people could claim white ethnicity based on their physical characteristics and were therefore allowed to become citizens. First-wave immigrants were predominately Christian, but an estimated 5 to 10 percent of them were Muslim. Most other immigrants from the Muslim-majority world—from the Middle East, Africa, and Asia—were considered non-white.

There were thriving Arab American communities in the East and the Midwest where there was work available in the textile and automotive factories. Dearborn, Michigan—home to the Ford Motor Company—had a large Arab American immigrant community, some of whom were Muslim. Today, the greater Detroit area (which includes the suburb of Dearborn) has one of the country's largest populations of Arab Americans. Other midwestern states like Iowa, Indiana, Illinois, and North Dakota also had sizeable Muslim communities. The first mosque in the United States was built in 1929 in Ross, North Dakota.

This historical photo shows the first mosque in America, which was built by Lebanese Muslims in 1929 in Ross, North Dakota.

Immigration Restrictions

Arab immigration slowed considerably beginning in 1917, when the first of a series of immigration laws was passed. Restricting immigration for "undesirable" groups has been a historically successful way of discriminating against people of other religions and nationalities. The United States government passed racist and xenophobic immigration legislation, much of which was not corrected until the 1960s American civil rights movement.

The 1917 Immigration Act, known as the Asiatic Barred Zone Act, instituted literacy tests, levied a tax on immigrants, and completely barred immigration from China, Southeast Asia, India, and Arabia. These restrictions affected most of the world's Muslim-majority nations and would not be lifted until the 1965 Immigration and Nationality Act.

The 1921 Emergency Quota Act limited the number of immigrants using quotas based on country of birth. Only 3 percent of the total number of foreign-born persons from a given country was allowed into the United States annually. The percentage was calculated using population data from the 1910 United States Census and favored immigrants from western Europe (someone was allowed in only if others of their nationality had already come to the United States). Things only worsened with the Immigration Act of 1924. Also known as the Johnson-Reed Act, this new immigration system used census data from 1890 and lowered the allowable percentage to 2 percent. This skewed things heavily in favor of western Europe, with the largest number of spots reserved for Germany, Great Britain, and Ireland—all predominately white, Christian nations. This was a form of de facto religious persecution, focused mostly on Roman Catholics from Italy and Jews from eastern Europe. The act also excluded all immigrants from Asia.

Anti-Catholic Sentiment

In the early days of America, Catholics were the biggest perceived threat to white Protestant America. There are differences between Protestant forms of Christianity and Catholicism, but one of the main causes of anti-Catholic sentiment in America was the Catholics' belief in the authority of the pope. The pope, called the bishop of Rome, is the leader of the Catholic Church and is identified by Catholics as the Vicar of Christ.

As far back as colonial times, there were laws that discriminated against Catholics. They were completely banned from some colonies, and their civil rights were severely restricted in others. They were a small minority for a long time, but in the mid-nineteenth century, a large number of Catholics immigrated to the United States from Ireland, Poland, and Germany. Many Protestant Americans believed that Catholics could never be truly American because their religion required their allegiance to the pope in Rome. This argument—that immigrants and American citizens of a minority religious group cannot be fully American—has been used throughout the nation's history and is still being used today against Muslims. For the nineteenth century Catholics, religious persecution manifested itself in much the same way it does today: prejudice, discrimination, civil rights violations, and violence.

Lyman Beecher, a prominent American Protestant (and the father of abolitionist author Harriet Beecher Stowe), was strongly anti-Catholic and preached in his sermons that the Catholic immigrants were part of a conspiracy to claim America for the pope. Shortly after one of his sermons in 1834, a mob burned down the Ursuline Convent in Boston. That same year, *Awful Disclosures of Maria Monk*—a false memoir about sexual deviance and infanticide in a Canadian convent—was published. This kind of thing perpetuated the idea that Catholics were corrupt and sinful. Some even believed Roman Catholicism to be the "Whore of Babylon" mentioned in the Bible.

The hostile environment and discrimination they faced—in 1922, Oregon passed a law requiring children to attend public schools, thereby making Catholic schools illegal—

Irish Catholic immigrants were the victims of job discrimination, as demonstrated by this historic Help Wanted sign.

made the Catholic community stronger in the face of this adversity, and they began to form their own institutions, such as Catholic schools, to serve the needs of the community. The irony of this is that the insular communities that Catholics formed as a result of hostility from non-Catholics served to make them more suspicious to outsiders who believed that they were corrupt and engaged in a sinister plot against America.

Anti-Catholic sentiment continued well into the twentieth century. The Ku Klux Klan of the early twentieth century was anti-Catholic in addition to being anti-black, anti-Semitic, anti-immigrant, and anti–organized labor. The Klan gained a lot of political power in the early 1900s. There were many Klan members who served as government officials at all levels: local, state, and federal. Among them was a Supreme Court justice, Hugo Black. At its peak during the Second Wave, there were eight million KKK members who would march openly in the streets promoting "America for Americans," and to the KKK, to be American was to be white, native-born, and Protestant.

One of the most notable illustrations of the political power of the KKK during the 1920s came during the 1924 Democratic National Convention at Madison Square Garden in New York City. The pro-KKK delegates from the South and West supported William G. McAdoo over Catholic candidate Al Smith. Physical and verbal fights broke out at the convention. To celebrate Independence Day, which fell during the convention, more than twenty thousand KKK members held a Fourth of July picnic across the Hudson River in New Jersey, where they donned their robes and hoods and burned crosses and effigies of Smith. After 103 ballots, the Democrats picked a compromise nominee, John W. Davis, who was a segregationist from the South. He lost the election to Calvin Coolidge. A constitutional lawyer, Davis defended segregation in 1954 before the Supreme Court in *Brown v. Board of Education of Topeka,* and lost.

Anti-Semitism

Between 1880 and 1920, Jews immigrated to the United States in large numbers, mostly from eastern and central Europe or Russia. During the period of mass immigration, there were violent anti-Jewish riots called **pogroms** taking place in their homelands, and many people were forced to flee in order to survive. Many of these refugees came to America for freedom and opportunity, but when they arrived, they faced widespread discrimination. Highly restrictive immigration laws passed in the 1920s directly affected Jewish refugees trying to flee continued persecution in Europe and Russia. The United States government actively turned away Jews during World War II, fearing that there may be communist spies among them.

Jewish Americans were targeted by the KKK; discriminated against in employment, housing, and club membership; and denied service in restaurants and hotels. Although anti-Semitism in America was nowhere near as virulent as it was in Europe, Jews in the United States did face violent religious persecution. One case—the 1915 lynching of Leo Frank, a Jewish factory manager—helped to expand and mobilize the newly created Anti-Defamation League (ADL). The ADL was created in 1913 by Jewish attorney Sigmund Livingston. Originally a grassroots organization run out of Livingston's office in Chicago, today the ADL is an international civil rights organization with offices across the nation and around the world. The ADL was created to fight discrimination,

This anti-Semitic cartoon is typical of the ugly stereotypes and caricatures ascribed to Jews in Europe and the United States in the early twentieth century.

including the negative portrayals of Jews in the media. Today, the ADL is also active in efforts to combat Islamophobia.

One of the most famous anti-Semites in American history is Henry Ford, founder of the Ford Motor Company and one of the most influential industrialists of the twentieth century. Ford owned a newspaper, the *Dearborn Independent*, in which he routinely published anti-Semitic content. Ford wrote a series of four articles that he printed and published separately as a pamphlet called *The International Jew*, which was available in all of his dealerships along with the *Independent*. Ford and other anti-Semites based a lot of their prejudice on a falsified document called *The Protocols of the Elders of Zion*, which claimed that Jewish leaders were plotting to take over the world by controlling the banks and the media. He reprinted parts of the *Protocols* in his paper and helped to spread negative Jewish stereotypes and conspiracy theories.

In the 1930s, as Adolf Hitler and the Nazis gained power in Europe and the United States was mired in the Great Depression, anti-Semitism continued on American soil. Influential Catholic radio priest Father Charles Coughlin, who had a nationwide audience through his affiliation with *CBS Broadcasting*, was doing his part to spread hate across America in the late 1930s. Like Ford, Coughlin believed that there was an international Jewish conspiracy and that Jewish bankers controlled international politics. He blamed the Jews for the war and defended the atrocities committed by Hitler and the Nazis. In 1938, with Coughlin's encouragement, a group of his listeners formed an anti-Semitic, pro-Nazi organization in New York City called Christian Front. Members routinely harassed Jewish people on the street, encouraged boycotts of Jewish-owned businesses, protested outside of radio stations that would not broadcast Coughlin's sermons, and distributed anti-Semitic literature, including Coughlin's own publication, *Social Justice*.

Second-Wave Arab Immigration

The goal of the United States during the Cold War (1947–1991) was to contain the spread of Soviet power and communist influence. It became the foreign policy of the United States to provide aid to countries that were threatened by Soviet forces and the spread of communism in exchange for those countries becoming US allies. The Middle East was an especially important region to control because it contained most of the world's oil supply. To this end, the United States forged diplomatic relations with both secular and Islamist nations in the Middle East. This new relationship ushered in the second wave of Arab immigration.

The United States altered its immigration policy to make exceptions for skilled professionals such as doctors, scientists, and engineers. Even though the quota system remained in place, the Immigration and Nationality Act of 1952 eliminated the Asiatic Barred Zone, which allowed a very diverse group of highly educated Arab immigrants to come to America. The second wave of immigration spanned from the 1950s to the 1960s. In addition to those from Syria and Lebanon, there were immigrants from Iraq, Egypt, Palestine, Jordan, and Yemen. As before, this wave was made up of both Christians and Muslims.

The second-wave Arab immigrants also included students from Arab countries who wanted to study at colleges and universities in the United States. Europe was devastated by World War II, and students who would have completed their higher education at European institutions went to the United States instead. Many of these students ended up staying after graduation and entering the American workforce.

The first Muslim Students Association (MSA) was formed in 1963 at the University of Illinois at Urbana-Champaign. The goal of the organization was for young Muslims to develop their cultural identity as Arab Americans and pursue an Islamic lifestyle in America. Arab students also began to take a more active interest in American politics.

Students from the first MSA went on to establish the Islamic Society of North America (ISNA) in 1982. The ISNA has become one of North America's largest Muslim organizations. Its stated goal is "to be an exemplary and unifying Islamic organization in North America that contributes to the betterment of the Muslim community and society at large" and "to foster the development of the Muslim community, interfaith relations, civic engagement, and better understanding of Islam."

In the midst of the second wave of immigration, the Islamic Center of Washington—a mosque and cultural center—was built on Embassy Row in Washington, DC, and opened in 1957. At that time, it was the largest mosque in the country. In his address at the dedication ceremony, President Dwight Eisenhower praised the Muslim American community and said, "America would fight with her whole strength for your right to have here your own church and worship according to your own conscience. This concept is indeed a part of America, and without that concept we would be something else than what we are."

Third-Wave Arab Immigration

The civil rights movement of the 1960s affected immigration law in the United States. The Immigration and Naturalization Act of 1965, also known as the Hart-Celler Act, abolished the quota system and banned discrimination based on race. The act provides the framework for the immigration policies in use today and has allowed millions of immigrants into the United States since it was passed. The third wave of Arab immigration began with this act and continues to the present day.

The third wave brought immigrants from many different countries, religions, and socioeconomic backgrounds. The percentage of Muslim Arabs was much higher than during previous waves, and there were a lot of war refugees from Lebanon, Iraq, and Palestine. The Lebanese Civil War, the conflict between Israel and Palestine, the Iranian Revolution, and the Gulf War drove people from their homelands. There were also a lot of professionals, entrepreneurs, and laborers who came from Egypt, Syria, Jordan, and Yemen. This diverse group settled in Arab American communities all over the United States.

Ali Stripped of His Title

Black Muslims came to represent black resistance and anti–Vietnam War sentiment, which at that time was the equivalent of being anti-American. Nowhere is this clearer than the case of Muhammad Ali. Born Cassius Clay, Ali was a boxer who won a gold medal for the US in the 1960 Olympic Games. He had a historically successful professional career, became the heavyweight champion of the world, and was considered an American hero. Cassius Clay shocked many

Boxing legend Muhammad Ali is pictured on December 2, 1990, with two released American hostages at Amman International Airport in Jordan.

when he joined the Nation of Islam in 1964 and changed his name to Muhammad Ali. The outspoken Ali became an activist against racism and war.

Ali refused to fight in the Vietnam War when he was drafted in 1967, claiming conscientious objector status. He said that his Muslim faith prohibited him from participating in the war. He also famously asked, "Why should they ask me to put on a uniform and go ten thousand miles from home and drop bombs and bullets on brown people in Vietnam while so-called Negro people in Louisville are treated like dogs and denied simple human rights?" Muhammad Ali was arrested and stripped of his boxing titles and license. He was convicted of draft dodging and sentenced to five years in prison. Ali remained free while appealing his conviction and spoke out against the war at colleges and universities.

The Supreme Court overturned Ali's conviction in 1971, shortly after he returned to boxing. In the 1970s, he began to study the Quran and made the Hajj pilgrimage to Mecca. Ali converted to mainstream Sunni Islam in the mid-1970s and rejected the NOI's black separatist ideology. Even before his retirement from boxing in 1981, Ali dedicated his time to humanitarian efforts around the globe. He was diagnosed with Parkinson's disease in 1984 but continued to travel and spread his message of peace. He went to Iraq in 1990, met with Saddam Hussein, and secured the release of US civilians taken hostage when Iraq invaded Kuwait. At the time of his death in 2016, he was one of the world's most famous and celebrated Muslim Americans.

African American Muslims

In the early twentieth century, African Americans and not Arab Americans were the public face of Islam in the United States. Many black Americans turned to Islam in the face of widespread racism and legal discrimination under Jim Crow laws that severely restricted their civil liberties. The Black Muslim movement was both religious and political and was seen as a major threat to white supremacy in America. The Nation of Islam (NOI), founded in Detroit in 1930, was the most prominent black-led Muslim organization at the time. Other black-led Sunni Islam groups were founded across the country, and in 1943 they held a convention in Philadelphia to form the Uniting Islamic Society of America.

The form of Islam practiced by the NOI was not traditional Sunni Islam. Its members followed the fundamental tenets of Islam, but traditional Muslims did not consider the NOI to be a true form of Islam. Their focus on separation of the races and their worship of NOI founder Wallace D. Fard as the messiah and his successor, Elijah Muhammad, as a prophet of God goes against traditional Islamic belief systems.

In the early 1940s, J. Edgar Hoover and the FBI launched a surveillance operation to investigate African American communities. They viewed black activists and African American Muslim organizations as dangerous and un-American and believed that they posed a threat to national security. The FBI arrested many African American leaders, including the NOI leader Elijah Muhammad. They found no actual evidence of treason against the United States but jailed many African American Muslims for refusing (on the basis of their Muslim faith) to register for the draft.

Nation of Islam membership grew and the group gained national prominence as the civil rights movement gained momentum during the 1950s and 1960s. The FBI ramped up its surveillance of the group (as well as others deemed "subversive") and launched a secret operation called COINTELPRO (Counter Intelligence Program). NOI leaders Elijah Muhammad and Malcolm X were targeted, as were black civil rights leaders outside the NOI (including Martin Luther King Jr., who was a vocal opponent of the Nation of Islam). The FBI used phone taps, informants, forged letters, and disinformation campaigns to discredit what they considered to be dangerous black nationalist hate groups.

Operation Boulder

At the 1972 Summer Olympics in Munich, West Germany, members of a Palestinian terrorist group that was a branch of the Palestine Liberation Organization, took eleven Israelis hostage. Two were killed immediately, and the rest were murdered during a botched rescue attempt. In response to this international incident, President Richard Nixon authorized FBI surveillance of Arab Americans, especially students who were openly critical of US foreign policy in the Middle East. Intelligence agencies targeted Arab Americans, non-native Arab immigrants, and non-Arab sympathizers, as well as relatives, friends, and employers of Arabs. There was no evidence of any criminal activity, just the assumption that they were linked to terrorist activity in Israel and Palestine because of Arab heritage or sympathies. This attack on their constitutional right to freedom of speech was initiated due to pressure from Zionists in the United States and in Israel who wanted to silence any verbal opposition or criticism.

International Conflict and Anti-Arab Discrimination

There was a great deal of discord in the Middle East during the twentieth century, and it led to discrimination against both Arab immigrants and native-born Arab Americans. The ongoing Israeli-Palestinian conflict and US foreign policy in the Middle East were—and continue to be—a major point of contention for Arab Americans who were sympathetic to the Palestinian people. There was a very negative portrayal of Arabs in the media after the 1967 Arab-Israeli War and the ongoing conflict in the region that led to oil embargos and shortages in 1973 and again in 1979. Arabs were generally depicted as villains. The men were either depicted as oil-rich billionaire sheiks, terrorist bombers, or religious fanatics. Arab women were either sexualized in harems of exotic belly dancers or were depicted as slaves to Arab men.

This only got worse after the Iranian Revolution of 1978–1979, when the king of Iran, Mohammad Reza Shah Pahlavi, was overthrown by supporters of the exiled Shia Muslim cleric Ayatollah Ruhollah Khomeini. Khomeini replaced the monarchy with a theocratic Islamic government and became the supreme leader of Iran. Khomeini declared that the United States, which had supported the shah and been an ally to Iran, was "the Great Satan" and an enemy of the new Islamic

Republic of Iran. Following the revolution, sixty-six Americans were taken hostage at the US Embassy in Tehran, causing a diplomatic crisis that lasted for 444 days until the last of the hostages were released on January 20, 1981.

As things went from bad to worse in the Middle East, terrorist violence escalated during the 1980s. There were several plane hijackings and bombings of US embassies in the Middle East. The media coverage of these incidents exacerbated existing prejudice against Arab Americans, and acts of politically motivated terrorism were linked to Islam in the American consciousness. Violence abroad led to anti-Arab violence at home.

In 1980, James Abourezk—the first Arab American US Senator—founded the American-Arab Anti-Discrimination Committee (ADC). The ADC is a civil rights organization created to fight anti-Arab racism and bigotry in America, which at the time of its founding was only getting worse. The ADC came under attack in 1985 when the Boston office was bombed. A few months later, after the hijacking of the cruise ship *Achille Lauro* in the Mediterranean Sea and the murder of a disabled Jewish American tourist named Leon Klinghoffer on board, a pipe bomb went off in the Santa Ana, California, office of the ADC, killing regional director Alex Odeh. Odeh was a known activist for Arab American civil rights and had received death threats before his murder.

Discrimination and attacks against Arab Americans surged during the Persian Gulf War (1990–1991). On August 2, 1990, Saddam Hussein and his Iraqi troops invaded and occupied Kuwait. Hussein refused the United

A bomb squad investigates the attack on the American-Arab Anti-Discrimination Committee office in Santa Ana, California. The blast killed Alex Odeh.

Nations order to withdraw from the country, and the United States, along with coalition forces, went to war against Iraq. The Persian Gulf War period saw an increase in attacks against Arab Americans. Things were so bad in Detroit that the mayor, Coleman Young, asked the governor to call in the National Guard to protect the city's substantial Muslim and Arab population.

Across the country, Arab-owned businesses and residences were vandalized, and both Muslim and non-Muslim Arab Americans were violently assaulted. Even before the combat phase of the Persian Gulf War began, anti-Arab hate crimes were so widespread that on September 24, 1990, President George H.W. Bush called for an end to the violence:

Death threats, physical attacks, vandalism, religious violence, and discrimination against Arab-Americans must end. These hate crimes have no place in a free society and we're not going to stand for them ... America is home to millions of Muslims who are free to live, work, and worship in accord with the traditions and teachings of Islam.

World Trade Center Bombing

On February 26, 1993, a truck containing a bomb exploded in a parking lot beneath the north tower of the World Trade Center in New York City, killing six people and injuring more than one thousand others. After an investigation, it was discovered that a terrorist cell based in and around New York City perpetrated the attack. The men directly involved in the bombing were attack leader Ramzi Yousef, Mohammed Salameh, Nidal Ayyad, Mahmoud Abouhalima, Ahmad Ajaj, and Abdul Rahman Yasin. Ramzi Yousef's uncle, Khalid Sheikh Mohammed, funded the bombing and would later play a central role in the September 11 attacks.

After the attack, the *New York Times* received a letter (later confirmed to have been sent by Nidal Ayyad) in which the conspirators called themselves the fifth battalion in the Liberation Army. Their stated goal for the attack was retaliation for the United States' political, economic, and military involvement in Israel. The letter demanded the United States stop all aid to Israel and, more generally, withdraw from the internal affairs of Middle Eastern countries, or the attacks on American soil would continue. Nowhere in the letter did it state that the attack was religiously motivated. In fact, it was very clearly stated that the bombing was intended to address the group's political grievances against the United States government.

The attack left innocent American Muslims and Arab Americans vulnerable to retaliation attacks. A 1995 ADC report stated that within three days, there were 222 incidents of reported harassment. These included incidents of police brutality, harassment at airports, verbal harassment via ethnic and religious slurs, discrimination in the workplace, and violent assaults.

Oklahoma City Bombing

On April 19, 1995, a bomb was detonated at the Alfred P. Murrah Federal Building in downtown Oklahoma City, killing 168 people. Almost immediately and without any concrete evidence, the media began to link the attack to foreign terrorists, specifically those from the Middle East. National news programs and papers jumped to the conclusion, via unnamed sources and those claiming to be terrorism experts, that the bombing must be the work of Middle Eastern terrorists. In the two days before the federal government confirmed it was not the work of foreigners, people assumed that the attack must be linked to the 1993 terrorist bombing of the World Trade Center in New York City, which had been carried out by a group of Islamic extremists. There were similarities in the method of attack: both were truck bombings.

The media's focus on the threat of foreign terrorism caused a wave of attacks against Muslim and Arab Americans in the days following the bombing. During CNN's coverage the day of the attack, anchor Frank Sesno reported that "a number of extremist Islamic groups have been traced to the Oklahoma area ... [and] they are among those who are being looked at very, very closely." The *New York Times* reported that "Middle Eastern groups have held meetings [in Oklahoma], and the city is home to at least three mosques." On the CBS Evening News, anchor Connie Chung reported that an unnamed government source told CBS that the attack had "Middle East terrorism written all over it." ABC News's national security correspondent, John McWethy, reported that intelligence sources and law enforcement officials said "this particular bombing probably has roots in the Middle East."

Domestic terrorist Timothy McVeigh leaves the Noble County Courthouse after being charged with the April 19, 1995, bombing of the Alfred P. Murrah Federal Building.

Even after it was discovered that the Oklahoma City bomber was a white US Army veteran from Western New York named Timothy McVeigh, CNN's Wolf Blitzer remarked, "There is still a possibility that there could have been some sort of connection to Middle East terrorism. One law enforcement source tells me that there's a possibility that [the suspects] may have been contracted out as freelancers." The fact that McVeigh and his accomplices were all white American men with no ties to Islam did not put an end to the anti-Muslim, anti-Arab rhetoric and prejudice following the domestic terrorist attack on Oklahoma City.

Innocent people across the nation were the victims of hate crimes that included verbal and physical attacks and discrimination, and many of their organizations, businesses, and mosques were vandalized. The morning after the bombing, a pregnant Muslim woman named Suhair Al Mosawi miscarried after someone threw bricks through the window of her Oklahoma City home. In Texas, a passing driver threatened an Islamic daycare center, and a mosque received threats by phone. There were hundreds more reported incidents of hate crimes in the days and weeks following the Oklahoma City attack, even though it was almost immediately proven to be an act of domestic terrorism, carried out by white Americans.

What the news media chose to overlook was the overwhelming response on the part of Muslim organizations and citizens. American Muslims condemned the attacks, and Muslim organizations raised money for the victims and held blood drives to help the injured. There was little to no coverage of the Muslim American community's sympathetic response and charity in the days following the attacks, nor were the hate crimes against innocent Americans deemed newsworthy. The media continued to speculate on the danger of foreign Islamic terrorism while ignoring the positive contributions of Muslim Americans at home.

Counterterrorism Legislation

In early 1995, a set of counterterrorism laws was drafted and introduced to Congress by then-senator Joe Biden. This bill contained provisions that would greatly expand the power of the federal government to fight terrorism. After the Oklahoma City bombing, the Omnibus Counterterrorism Act of 1995 was passed. Among other provisions, this act made it legal to deport non-citizens based on secret evidence, allowed the government to detain people indefinitely and without trial based on secret evidence, and made it a crime to contribute to any charity or organization deemed a "terrorist organization" by the president.

This set of laws was disproportionately used against Muslims and Arab Americans. Basic civil rights guaranteed by the Constitution—such as the right to due process of law and protection against unlawful search and seizure—were stripped from many individuals who were considered guilty by association. This legislation served as a precursor to the even more restrictive USA PATRIOT Act passed in the wake of the September 11 attacks.

TWO

The Day the World Changed

Although Islamophobia certainly existed in America before the twenty-first century, there was no single event that catalyzed more hatred and prejudice against Muslims than the terrorist attacks of September 11, 2001. It was a collective national trauma that set off the War on Terror abroad and the war against Muslims at home.

There have been three major waves of Islamophobic persecution and prejudice against both Muslim Americans and non-Muslim Arab Americans. The first came immediately after the September 11 attacks. The second wave occurred after the 2008 election of Barack Obama as president and a series of smaller-scale attacks that followed. The third wave is currently under way and only gaining steam as a new enemy—the Islamic State (known as ISIS or ISIL)—carries out terrorist attacks against Muslims and non-Muslims around the world.

Opposite: The north and south towers of the World Trade Center in New York City burn on September 11, 2001, after commercial airliners crashed into the buildings.

America Under Attack

At 8:45 a.m. on September 11, 2001, American Airlines Flight 11 crashed into the north tower of the World Trade Center in New York City. Eighteen minutes later, at 9:03 a.m., United Airlines Flight 175 crashed into the south tower. At 9:37 a.m., American Airlines Flight 77 crashed into the Pentagon in Washington, DC. A fourth plane, United Airlines Flight 93, crashed in a field near Shanksville, Pennsylvania. All four planes were commercial airliners containing civilian passengers that had been hijacked by suicide bombers from the terrorist group al-Qaeda. This coordinated attack was the worst on American soil since the World War II bombing of Pearl Harbor in 1941.

The collapse of the Twin Towers of the World Trade Center, which could not withstand the heat from the ignited jet fuel, is an image that is burned into the American consciousness. There were many thousands of civilian and first responder injuries, and nearly three thousand people died, making the 9/11 attacks the deadliest ever on American soil. Many of the casualties were emergency service workers who perished when the towers fell. The number would have been even higher if Flight 93 had made it to its intended target, which is thought to have been either the US Capitol or the White House. Instead, the passengers (who had heard the news of the other hijackings) bravely fought back against the terrorists and crashed the plane in a rural area, where there were no residents to be injured.

First responders flee the cloud of debris that blanketed lower Manhattan after the collapse of the first tower. The second tower came down shortly after.

Fifteen of the nineteen al-Qaeda operatives responsible for carrying out the attacks were from Saudi Arabia; the others were from the United Arab Emirates (two), Lebanon (one), and Egypt (one). They were funded and trained by known terrorist Osama bin Laden, a longtime enemy of the United States. The attacks on iconic American landmarks were meant to demonstrate al-Qaeda's hatred of the United States.

The television news coverage showed the events of September 11 live as they unfolded. For days and weeks afterward, graphic images of the attacks and the collapse of the towers, people jumping from the burning buildings, debris and ash blanketing downtown Manhattan, and recovery efforts at **Ground Zero** were shown on a constant loop. There were interviews with first responders, eyewitnesses, and victims' family members. Broadcast networks suspended programming and reported with no commercial breaks.

As with the 1993 bombing, news networks relied on government sources and terrorism experts for information on the ongoing investigation. The onslaught of disturbing imagery coupled with discussions of Islamic terrorist threats created an atmosphere of fear and anxiety that was devastating to the Arab American community. The media's constant use of the word "Islamic" before words suggesting terrorism or extremism was (and continues to be) offensive to many Muslims as it reinforced the Islamophobic idea that Islam is inherently violent.

The White House Responds

On September 14, Congress authorized the use of military force against those responsible for the attacks. On September 20, President George W. Bush addressed Congress and the nation about al-Qaeda, bin Laden, and the Taliban regime in Afghanistan. In his address, Bush made the following demands of the Taliban: (1) deliver to the United States all al-Qaeda leaders hiding in Afghanistan; (2) release American and foreign national prisoners; (3) protect foreign journalists, diplomats, and humanitarian workers in Afghanistan; (4) close all terrorist training camps and allow the United States full access to former training sites; and (5) hand over all terrorists and their support structure to the appropriate authorities.

Bush went on to specifically dissociate the worldwide Muslim community from the extremists responsible for the 9/11 attacks:

We respect your faith. [Islam is] practiced freely by many millions of Americans and by millions more in countries that America counts as friends. Its teachings are good and peaceful, and those who commit evil in the name of Allah blaspheme the name of Allah. The terrorists are traitors to their own faith, trying, in effect, to hijack Islam itself. The enemy of America is not our many Muslim friends. It is not our many Arab friends. Our enemy is a radical network of terrorists and every government that supports them.

Speaking from the Washington Islamic Center in Washington, DC, a few days earlier on September 17, Bush had also denounced violence against Muslims when he said, "Muslims are doctors, lawyers, law professors, members of the military, entrepreneurs, shopkeepers, moms and dads, and they need to be treated with respect."

In the early days after the 9/11 attacks, President Bush repeatedly asked Americans to uphold the country's values during a time of crisis, especially the American constitutional right not to be discriminated against for race, ethnicity, or religious faith. But while Bush was instructing the people to uphold these principles, he was also presenting the attack in an overly simplistic way that undermined his message of unity. In his address to the nation, Bush said:

Americans are asking, "Why do they hate us?" They hate what they see right here in this chamber: a democratically elected government. Their leaders are self-appointed. They hate our freedoms: our freedom of religion, our freedom of speech, our freedom to vote and assemble and disagree with each other.

The reality of the situation was much more complex than this. The president's statement and the media coverage that followed presented the attack as simply a hatred of American freedom. This was misleading and ignored the historical and political context in which these attacks occurred.

At the time of the 9/11 attacks, the average American knew very little about the history between the United States and the people who organized and carried out the attacks. They also did not know much, if anything, about Islam as a religion. There is a long and complicated history of US involvement in the Middle East that led up to the events of September 11, 2001, and while there is no excuse for any act of terrorism, to ignore the historical context of the relationship between the United States and Islamic fundamentalist groups is an oversimplification. It is easy for Islamophobes to vilify Islam as a religion while ignoring the political and economic factors that fuel acts of terrorism.

US in the Soviet-Afghan War (1979– 1989)

Afghanistan was in a strategic position geographically during the later years of the Cold War because it is located between the Middle East and the Soviet Union. In late December 1979, the Soviet Union sent troops into Afghanistan and took military and political control of most of the country, including the capital of Kabul. At that time, the country was plagued by civil war between the pro-Soviet, pro-communist government and the anti-communist Muslims who called themselves the **mujahideen**.

The literal translation of this Arabic word is "those engaging in **jihad**" (which itself means "struggle" or "striving"). Jihad is a complex theological concept that is often misunderstood and twisted by non-Muslims. In America and the West, it has come to mean "holy war" largely due to Muslims like the mujahideen and other extremist groups who use the word to mean armed struggle against enemies of the faith. While this is one interpretation of jihad, it is not the only interpretation, and it is certainly not the interpretation of the majority of American Muslims. Contrary to what some people believe, jihad is not one of the pillars of Islam.

The Afghan war served as a **proxy war**: a conflict between two nations—in this case, the United States and the Soviet Union—where they do not engage with each other directly but instead support combatants who represent their interests. Under President Ronald Reagan, the United States supported the mujahideen through a covert CIA operation called Operation Cyclone. For a decade, the US provided money and arms such as Stinger antiaircraft missile launchers, which were portable and able to take down Soviet helicopters. With the assistance of the government of Pakistan and their Inter-Services Intelligence (ISI), the United States was able to assist and arm the mujahideen against the Soviets.

The goal of this was to stop the spread of Soviet influence into the Middle East, and to do so the US government fully supported the Afghan rebel fighters. The war resulted in mass

Covert Operation

Charles Wilson was a nondescript congressman from Texas known for his wild lifestyle—he was nicknamed Good Time Charlie—until he helped fund the largest covert CIA operation in US history.

Wilson was a fervent anti-communist; he spent time at the Pentagon in intelligence. He evaluated the Soviet Union's nuclear forces. Elected to congress in 1972, he was appointed to the Defense Appropriations subcommittee, which funds CIA operations, shortly after the Soviet invasion of Afghanistan in December 1979. Using his influence, he made deals to increase aid to Afghanistan from a few million dollars to about $750 million per year by the end of the 1980s.

After the Soviets pulled out of Afghanistan, the president of Pakistan credited Wilson with winning the war. A book titled *Charlie Wilson's War* was written in 2003, and the book was turned into a movie starring Tom Hanks and Julia Roberts in 2007.

civilian casualties and created around five million refugees, most of whom went to Pakistan and Iraq. It also destroyed a lot of Afghanistan's infrastructure and left the country with no central, organized leadership (a situation known as a **power vacuum**). Once the Soviets were defeated and the Cold War was drawing to a close, the United States withdrew all funding, leaving Afghanistan devastated and with no money to rebuild. In this chaotic postwar environment, Muslim extremist groups like the Taliban and al-Qaeda emerged.

Osama bin Laden and al-Qaeda

During the Soviet-Afghan war, many Arab Muslims came from around the region to join the fight against the Soviet occupation. One of these men was Osama bin Laden, a wealthy man from Saudi Arabia. He joined the resistance and used his connections to help fund the mujahideen in the battle against the Soviets. Bin Laden was not a fighter; he used his wealth and connections to create a global recruitment network to bring young Muslim men from around the world to Afghanistan and train them for war. Near the end of the Soviet occupation, in 1988, bin Laden formed a militant Islamist group called al-Qaeda.

After the Soviet withdrawal, bin Laden returned home to Saudi Arabia as a war hero and attempted to expand his organization. When Iraq invaded Kuwait in 1990, bin Laden offered al-Qaeda fighters to help Saudi Arabia protect its territory, but the Saudi royal family rejected the offer. Instead, it allowed US troops and coalition allies to base themselves in Saudi Arabia during the Persian Gulf War. This angered bin Laden, who believed that foreign troops should not be permitted on Islam's sacred ground near the holy cities of Mecca and Medina. Bin Laden became openly hostile and was exiled from Saudi Arabia.

He moved al-Qaeda's operations to Sudan and began to wage a violent jihad against the West. Al-Qaeda's first attack directed toward the United States occurred in 1992, when he orchestrated the bombing of multiple hotels in Aden, Yemen, where he believed (incorrectly) that American troops were staying on their way to Somalia. In 1996, bin Laden moved al-Qaeda's base of operations to Afghanistan, where they had the protection of the Taliban.

In August 1996, without any recognized religious authority to do so, bin Laden issued his first **fatwa** (an Islamic legal pronouncement). In his "Declaration of Jihad on the Americans Occupying the Country of the Two Sacred Places," bin Laden declared holy war against the United States and Israel. He issued another in 1998, and a few months later, on August 7, 1998, al-Qaeda bombed the US embassies in Nairobi, Kenya, and Dar es Salaam, Tanzania. Hundreds were killed and thousands injured in these attacks, and the FBI placed bin Laden on the Most Wanted list. The CIA hunted for bin Laden but was unable to capture him, and he continued to plan and fund terrorist attacks. On October 12, 2000, al-Qaeda was responsible for the suicide bombing of the USS *Cole*, a US Navy ship off the coast of Yemen. Less than a year later, the Twin Towers came down.

The USA PATRIOT Act

On October 26, 2001, President Bush signed the USA PATRIOT Act into law. "USA PATRIOT" stands for Uniting and Strengthening America by Providing Appropriate Tools Required to Intercept and Obstruct Terrorism. This legislation gave the US government easy access to electronic surveillance as well as medical records, bank and credit records, library records, travel records, phone and internet records, and other private, personal information. It also allowed for the indefinite detention and deportation of immigrants and other

The wreck of the USS *Cole* is towed out of Aden in Yemen on October 12, 2000.

non-citizens who are suspected of terrorist associations. This could be something as simple as donating money to a charity that the government has labeled a terrorist organization.

There was very little required oversight by the courts, and the FBI was allowed to conduct searches and surveillance operations without a court order. Instead of search warrants, they issued National Security Letters (NSLs) that allowed the government to conduct secret surveillance operations. The federal government kept any information obtained via NSLs, even if it revealed no evidence of wrongdoing. The PATRIOT Act also allowed "sneak and peek" searches in which law enforcement agencies are permitted to conduct searches of a home or office without the occupant knowing until after the fact.

Many people felt that the provisions in the PATRIOT Act were unconstitutional, violating (among other things) the Fourth Amendment protection against unlawful search and seizure. Its effectiveness in combating terrorism has also been questioned. According to the American Civil Liberties Union (ACLU), between 2003 and 2006 the FBI issued 192,499 NSLs, all of which resulted in only one conviction related to terrorism.

The act has also been used by law enforcement to conduct investigations completely unrelated to terrorist activity. The ACLU reported that between 2003 and 2005, the FBI made fifty-three criminal referrals to prosecutors based on information from 143,074 NSLs. Of those fifty-three criminal cases, seventeen were related to money laundering, seventeen to immigration, and nineteen to fraud; none of them were related to acts of terrorism. Sneak-and-peek searches were also more likely to be used for crimes unrelated to terrorism. In 2010, less than 1 percent of sneak-and-peek searches were terror-related; most of the searches (76 percent) were drug related.

Department of Homeland Security

On October 8, 2001, in direct response to the September 11 attacks, President Bush issued Executive Order 13228, which created the Office of Homeland Security. This served as the predecessor to the Department of Homeland Security established the following year by the Homeland Security Act of 2002. This was the largest reorganization of government agencies since the creation of the Department of Defense during the Cold War. Twenty-two agencies from other departments were absorbed into the Department of Homeland Security, including agencies in charge of border patrol and immigration. The Department of Homeland Security includes many of the organizations responsible for enforcing the PATRIOT Act.

The Department of Homeland Security was also responsible for the color-coded advisory system that was introduced by the Bush administration in March 2002. The Homeland Security

This December 28, 2009, photo shows a national threat advisory sign outside the security screening area at Baltimore Washington International Airport.

Advisory System was used to inform the public of current terrorist threat levels against the United States.

For years, the threat levels remained mostly at orange (high) and yellow (elevated); the lower levels blue (guarded) and green (low) were never used. The system did little except keep the American people in a constant state of fear. One instance when the terror threat was raised from yellow to orange was linked to the religious period of Hajj (the pilgrimage to Mecca) in February 2003.

The War on Terror

On October 7, 2001, the United States launched the first stage in the global War on Terror that continues to the present day. Operation Enduring Freedom was carried out to depose the Taliban in Afghanistan and capture al-Qaeda operatives hiding there. It began with a series of air strikes on Taliban strongholds in Afghanistan and a ground war waged by a coalition of forces including the Northern Alliance—the Taliban's enemies in Afghanistan. The Taliban suffered many losses, and by December 2001, the Taliban regime in Afghanistan had collapsed. Taliban and al-Qaeda operatives went underground, hiding in remote areas of Afghanistan and in nearby Pakistan. Despite the early victory, the war in Afghanistan would last for more than a decade.

The second stage of the war was more controversial. When America went to war with Iraq, it did so on the claims that Iraq and Saddam Hussein had weapons of mass destruction (WMDs) and that Iraq was harboring and supporting al-Qaeda terrorists. The Iraq War began on March 20, 2003, with Operation Iraqi Freedom. An air and ground campaign lasted until May 1, when President Bush famously declared an end to major combat operations in Iraq. This has become known as the "Mission Accomplished" speech in which President Bush prematurely declared an end to the Iraq War, which would last until the final troop withdrawal in December 2011. In his speech, Bush declared victory over the Iraqi dictator Saddam Hussein and his regime but made it clear that there was still work to do in fighting terrorist cells in Iraq, as well as locating Iraq's WMDs.

Things quickly deteriorated as it became clearer that Iraq did not possess weapons of mass destruction. Coupled with the instability in the country and the Iraqi insurgency forces fighting the US-led occupation, the war became incredibly unpopular as it stretched on for eight years after victory was declared in 2003. Billions of dollars were spent on the war, thousands of American troops lost their lives, and by some estimates there were almost 150,000 civilian casualties in Iraq.

America's reputation was further damaged when reports of human rights violations against Iraqi prisoners surfaced.

At Abu Ghraib prison near Baghdad, American military personnel abused and tortured Iraqi prisoners. Graphic pictures of the American soldiers gleefully committing human rights violations against prisoners of war circulated around the globe. There were further reports of atrocities at facilities in Afghanistan and Guantanamo Bay, Cuba, including torture of prisoners as an interrogation tactic. These so-called enhanced interrogation techniques were authorized by the CIA. They included waterboarding, a technique that simulates the experience of drowning.

Between human rights abuses of prisoners, the fact that no WMDs were found in Iraq, and the lack of any evidence connecting Saddam Hussein to the 9/11 attacks, the Iraq War became a controversial political issue in the 2004 presidential election. President Bush's popularity was waning, as was support for the war. In this environment, Islamophobia was used strategically to drum up support for the war. The Islamophobic rationale for a continued presence in Iraq was that the United States must defend itself against Islamic terrorists (implies Islam is an inherently violent religion), it needed to introduce democratic governments to Muslim-majority countries (implies Islam is incompatible with democracy), and that America must rescue Muslim women (implies Islam is a repressive and misogynist religion).

Second-Wave Islamophobia

The second wave of Islamophobia in America began in 2008 when Barack Hussein Obama was elected president of the United States. A black president with an Arab-sounding name was something very new and very different for America, and some people did not take kindly to it. Even before Obama was elected, he was being smeared as a "secret Muslim," as if being Muslim is by its very nature a bad thing. There were conspiracy theories about his citizenship and demands that he produce his birth certificate to prove he was born in Hawaii and not Kenya, where his father was from. These questions about Obama's religion, citizenship, and loyalty to the United States did not go away over the course of his eight years in office. A poll taken in 2015 stated that 29 percent of Americans believed that Obama was a Muslim and that he was lying about his Christian faith.

Obama inherited the wars in the Middle East and took office during the worst economic crisis the nation had seen since the Great Depression. As history shows, in times of crisis, people tend to lash out at groups they perceive as "other," and Muslims and Arab Americans were the new face of the enemy. Things escalated after the 2009 shooting at the Fort Hood army base in Texas. On November 5, 2009, US Army major and psychiatrist Nidal Hasan shot and killed thirteen people and injured more than thirty others at Fort Hood's Soldier Readiness Processing Center where he worked. Hasan was born in Virginia to Palestinian immigrant parents. He had a history of mental instability and behavioral problems before the attacks and had become radicalized after the death of his parents. Hasan represented America's new worst fear: the homegrown terrorist had replaced the foreign terrorist.

Not long after, on May 1, 2010, there was an attempted terrorist car bombing in New York City's iconic Times Square. The attack was thwarted because street vendors in the area noticed smoke coming from an SUV parked in the busy tourist area and alerted the police. Luckily the bomb had malfunctioned and the bomb squads were able to remove it without any injuries. The would-be-bomber turned out to be a Pakistani immigrant named Faisal Shahzad. Shahzad had been in America since 1999 and became a citizen in 2009—the same year he trained with the Taliban in Pakistan. Shahzad admitted to the attacks and claimed that they were in retaliation for US drone strikes in Pakistan, where his family still lived.

Second-wave Islamophobia was thriving at the beginning of the second decade of the twenty-first century and was only helped along in 2013 when a bomb went off at the Boston Marathon, killing three people and injuring more than 250 others. The bombers were brothers from the North Caucasus, Tamerlan and Dzhokhar Tsarnaev. They had

no direct ties to terrorist organizations and were radicalized mostly via the internet, including *Inspire*, the online English-language publication of al-Qaeda in Yemen.

This NYPD photo shows part of a homemade bomb rigged to explode in an SUV in New York City's Times Square on May 1, 2010.

The Rise of ISIS and the Third Wave

The Islamic State in Iraq and Syria (ISIS) had as its origins the instability caused by the War in Iraq. Former leader Saddam Hussein was part of the Sunni minority in the country and had oppressed the Shia majority population during his rule. After he was deposed, the Shias took over and oppressed the Sunnis. The Shias and the Sunnis are the largest branches of Islam. The US peacekeeping attempts in Iraq failed as the Sunni rebel uprising began. Members of al-Qaeda as well as members of the former Sunni military fought against US and coalition troops and the new Iraqi state security forces in the civil war of 2006–2007.

The lack of stability and security in Iraq made it a perfect breeding ground for terrorism. The war had left a power vacuum in Iraq and had not solved any of the country's previous problems under Hussein's dictatorship: the Iraqi people were still plagued by instability, insecurity, and inequality. A terrorist group called the Islamic State in Iraq (ISI), which was allied with al-Qaeda, started to gain power and territory in Iraq during the chaos of civil war. Their goals were to expel US and coalition forces and create an Islamic caliphate in Iraq. ISI had financial support from terrorists in oil-rich Saudi Arabia and took control of large parts of northern Iraq near the Syrian border.

ISI was a relatively small group of militants until a series of events called the Arab Spring began in 2010. The Arab Spring was a movement in parts of the Middle East and North Africa led by educated young people who were unable to find work in their struggling economies. These people began to organize and protest against their corrupt governments. The wave of demonstrations began in Tunisia and soon spread to Libya, Egypt, Yemen, Bahrain, and Syria. The Arab Spring was successful in Tunisia but elsewhere led to violence and ongoing instability in the region, especially in Syria.

Syrian president Bashar al-Assad refused to resign, and in March 2011, Assad's forces fired on peaceful protestors. Within months, the country was embroiled in civil war, and extremists from around the region—including ISI—traveled to Syria to join the rebels. ISI already had a large base and fighters in Iraq and controlled areas on the Syrian border. Some of the Syrian rebel forces defected to join the group, now calling itself the Islamic State in Iraq and Syria (ISIS). The group is alternately referred to as ISIL (Islamic State in Iraq and the Levant).

ISIS was so violent and radical that even al-Qaeda denounced them and withdrew support. They have become the wealthiest terrorist organization in the world, with millions of dollars in financing coming from seized oil fields in northern Iraq and Syria and captured banks, among other things. ISIS is also well armed, having seized US-supplied military equipment in Iraq after defeating the Iraqi army and taking many of Iraq's major cities. ISIS continues to expand its reach and commit atrocities all around the globe. It is particularly effective at using social media and the internet as a recruitment tool, and with no shortage of disaffected young men in the region and around the globe, it shows no signs of stopping.

THREE

The Last "Acceptable" Prejudice

For Muslim Americans, life was fundamentally and irrevocably different after 9/11. Muslims and those mistaken for Muslims were subject to discriminatory practices that were considered not only acceptable but necessary for national security in a post-9/11 America. The laws and procedures enacted after the attacks both allowed and encouraged institutionalized discrimination and racism against Muslim Americans, non-Muslim Arabs, and Sikhs.

Post-9/11 Hate Crimes

There was a wave of violent Islamophobic attacks, both verbal and physical, in the days and weeks after 9/11. Within hours, people across America were committing hate crimes against those whom they perceived as Muslims; this included non-Muslim Arabs and Sikhs. Islamic cultural centers and mosques, as well as businesses owned and/or operated by Arab Americans, were also targeted.

Opposite: The Islamic Center of America in Dearborn, Michigan, was vandalized on January 23, 2007, in a religiously motivated hate crime.

Even though early reports from the media had no confirmed factual information about the terrorists' identities, there was a rash of hate crimes that started mere hours after the morning's attack. In Ronkonkoma, New York, about 50 miles (80 km) from downtown Manhattan, a man named Brian Harris was charged with a hate crime after he threatened an Arab American gas station clerk with a pistol and shouted ethnic slurs. On September 12, in South Huntington, New York (also near Manhattan), Adam Lang, a seventy-six-year-old man, was charged with reckless endangerment after he attempted to hit a Pakistani woman with his car in a mall parking lot. According to police, Lang jumped out of the car and screamed that he was "doing this for his country."

Incidents of violence were not limited to New York or the surrounding area. All around the country, people were lashing out at innocent people whom they associated with the attacks based purely on their appearance, ethnicity, and/or religious affiliation. On September 12, thirty-one-year-old Michael Herrick set fire to Curry in a Hurry, a restaurant owned and operated by a Pakistani family in Salt Lake City, Utah. On September 13, forty-nine-year-old Andrew Holden threatened to bomb a food store owned by an Arab American in Chicago, Illinois. According to police, Holden threatened the owner and said, "I've got a bomb in this bag and I'm going to blow this store up like you Arabs blew up the World Trade Center." According to a report prepared by the Southern Poverty Law Center, an organization that monitors hate groups and crimes in the United States, within the first year after the attacks, there were more than fifty incidents reported in the news. That number doesn't take into account the incidents that the media did not cover.

There were also many attacks on mosques and Islamic community centers around the country. In Irving, Texas, someone shot at a window of the Islamic Center of Irving in the early morning hours of September 12. No one was injured, but the attack caused thousands of dollars in damage and deeply disturbed the Muslim community that had, the day before, organized a blood drive and a donation fund for victims. On September 17, Eric Richley drove his car into a mosque in Parma, Ohio. No one was injured, but the attack caused $100,000 in damages. Although Richley was intoxicated at the time, it was not an accident, and he later pled guilty to ethnic intimidation and vandalism.

Murdering Innocents

The first American casualty of Islamophobic violence after September 11 was not even a Muslim. On September 15, a forty-nine-year-old Sikh man named Balbir Singh Sodhi was fatally shot outside his gas station in Mesa, Arizona. Sodhi was an immigrant from India who moved to the United States in 1989. As a male of the Sikh faith, Sodhi wore a traditional beard and turban. The murderer, Frank Roque, mistook Sodhi for a Muslim because of his appearance. Roque shot Sodhi to death from his truck. He also fired at a Lebanese man at another gas station and at the home of an Afghan family, but no one else was injured. At Roque's trial, the prosecution stated that on September 11, Roque told an employee at an Applebee's that he was going to "go out and shoot some

A family visits the Mesa, Arizona, memorial to the murdered Balbir Singh Sodhi.

towel-heads" and that he told a coworker, "We should round them all up and kill them. We should kill their children, too, because they'll grow up to be like their parents."

Also on September 15, Waqar Hasan, an immigrant from Pakistan, was shot and killed in his convenience store in Dallas, Texas. A few days later, the killer, Mark Stroman, went on to shoot a Bangladeshi American man, Rais Bhuiyan, at another Texas convenience store, but Bhuiyan survived. On October 4, Stroman killed forty-nine-year-old Vasudev Patel, a Hindu immigrant from India, at a gas station in Mesquite, Texas, and was finally apprehended by police. Stroman was a self-proclaimed "Arab Slayer" taking revenge for the 9/11 attacks, but all three of his victims were from South Asia, and only two—Hasan and Bhuiyan—were Muslim.

Stroman was ultimately convicted and sentenced to death in Texas. However, despite the fact that Stroman attempted to murder him, Bhuiyan tried to save his would-be killer from the death penalty. Bhuiyan's Muslim faith taught him to forgive and that saving one life is the same as saving all of humanity. In the end, Bhuiyan's efforts to save Stroman failed, but his actions greatly affected Stroman's beliefs about Muslims in his final days. In an interview with the *New York Times* shortly before his scheduled execution, Stroman said, "[Bhuiyan's] deep Islamic beliefs gave him the strength to forgive the un-forgivable ... that is truly inspiring to me, and should be an example for us all. The hate, has to stop, we are all in this world together."

NYPD Surveillance Program

In August 2011, the Associated Press began publishing reports that the New York Police Department (NYPD) had been conducting a program of institutionalized religious and ethnic profiling and surveillance of the Muslim community in New York City as well as in the nearby states of New Jersey, Connecticut, and Pennsylvania. Reporters Matt Apuzzo, Adam Goldman, Chris Hawley, and Eileen Sullivan won the 2012 Pulitzer Prize for Investigative Journalism for their in-depth exposé of the NYPD's secret surveillance programs, which began in 2002 after the September 11 attacks that devastated Lower Manhattan.

With the help of the CIA, the NYPD's Intelligence Division created the Demographics Unit (renamed the Zone Assessment Unit in 2010). This unit places undercover Arab and South Asian detectives (known as **rakers**) into Muslim American community spaces to gather intelligence. These covert surveillance operations on American citizens take place in mosques, community centers, bookstores, restaurants, nightclubs, cafes, and other "Muslim hotspots"—any location with large Muslim and Arab populations.

There is also a specialized group known as the Terrorist Interdiction Unit (TIU) that employs informants within Muslim communities to gather information. They are often referred to as **mosque crawlers** because they target Muslim houses of worship, reporting back to the police what the imam said in his sermon as well as the names of worshippers in attendance. The Associated Press reported the story of one of these informants, nineteen-year-old Shamiur Rahman, a Bangladeshi American. Rahman was recruited from jail, where he was being held on his third misdemeanor drug charge.

A community center and hookah lounge is among the many Arab businesses on Steinway Street in the Astoria section of Queens, New York.

He was given leniency and paid by the NYPD to engage in "create and capture" tactics of information gathering: he was encouraged to start ("create") conversations with others about jihad and terrorism and then report ("capture") the response to the police.

Rahman spied on many mosques as well as members of the Muslim Student Association at Manhattan's John Jay College of Criminal Justice. He became friends with members of the student group while reporting their names and activities to the NYPD. Rahman said that he wanted to please his handler at the NYPD, and he would bring up controversial topics like the attack on the US consulate in Libya knowing they would provoke strong reactions. He said that it was easy to take statements out of context and that he was just "trying to get money" and was "playing the game." Eventually, Rahman felt too guilty taking money for spying on innocent members of the Muslim American community and he confessed to his friends on Facebook. Even though he originally believed that he was helping to fight terrorism, Rahman now believes that his activities were "detrimental to the Constitution."

The NYPD surveillance programs did much more harm than good. They did not result in any concrete intelligence or terror prosecutions. Instead, they created an environment of mistrust in Muslim American communities. The constant surveillance at houses of worship severely restricted both freedom of religion and freedom of speech. Many Muslim Americans began to feel as if they could not worship freely at mosques and decided to start worshipping privately in their homes to avoid being harassed or wrongly accused. They also felt pressure to change their appearance (clothes, head scarfs, facial hair, etc.) so as not to be easy targets. Imams felt as if they needed to censor sermons and record them so that the authorities would not take statements out of context.

Even outside the mosque, members of the community are wary of engaging in any sort of political activism or speech that could be construed as radical by someone listening in. This environment of fear violates the constitutional rights of American citizens to freely practice their religion and speak their minds, yet this type of religious and ethnic profiling is not only acceptable but actively encouraged by law enforcement. This kind of anxiety about freedom of speech and religion is not limited to the New York area. Muslims all around the country feel they have been stripped of their constitutional rights and freedoms.

Radicalization Theory

In 2007, the NYPD Intelligence Division created a document called "Radicalization in the West: The Homegrown Threat," in which it claimed that there are four steps to the "radicalization" of American Muslims that result in their becoming homegrown terrorists. The NYPD report defines the stages as follows:

(1) **Pre-radicalization.** The first stage is "the point of origin for individuals before they begin this progression" and includes all young Muslim men from American middle class or immigrant families. These individuals "began

as 'unremarkable'—they had 'ordinary' jobs, had lived 'ordinary' lives and had little, if any criminal history."

(2) **Self-identification.** The second stage includes Muslims who "begin to explore **Salafi** Islam" and "associate themselves with like-minded individuals." This "religious seeking" can be triggered by traumatic life events such as losing one's job, the death of a loved one, or being a victim of discrimination and racism. Signs of self-identification include "giving up cigarettes, drinking, gambling and urban hip-hop gangster clothes," "wearing traditional Islamic clothing, growing a beard," and "becoming involved in social activism and community issues."

(3) **Indoctrination.** The third stage is when "an individual progressively intensifies his beliefs [and] wholly adopts jihadi-Salafi ideology." At the indoctrination stage, the individual accepts the "religious-political worldview that justifies, legitimizes, encourages, or supports violence against anything *kufr*, or un-Islamic, including the West, its citizens, its allies, or other Muslims whose opinions are contrary to the extremist agenda." Signs of indoctrination are withdrawal from the mosque and politicization of beliefs.

(4) **Jihadization.** The final stage is when individuals "accept their individual duty to participate in jihad and self-designate themselves as holy

warriors or mujahedeen. Ultimately, the group will begin operational planning for jihad or a terrorist attack." Signs of jihadization include traveling abroad, engaging in "'Outward Bound'-like activities" like camping, white-water rafting, paintball games, target shooting, and increased internet activity that helps reinforce their extremist ideology and plan the inevitable attacks.

Just looking at these four stages and some of the activities designated as red flags shows how easy it is for ordinary American Muslims to become suspects. It also demonstrates the shift in focus from foreign terrorists to the new threat of homegrown terrorism: American citizens who, by nature of their association with Islam, become radicalized and dangerous.

According to this theory, a Muslim simply following the rules of their religion and dressing in a traditional way is already a suspect on the road to becoming a full-fledged terrorist. Muslim Americans exercising their right to free speech by becoming politically and socially active in their communities are considered radicals. Under this rubric, a Muslim who withdraws from his or her mosque to pray more safely at home or in small groups elsewhere is suspect. Wholesome activities like camping and paintball, which would never be viewed as suspicious for other groups of Americans, are for Muslims a sign of imminent terrorist activity.

This system can create legalized discrimination against the Muslim American community.

The "Ground Zero Mosque" Controversy

In December 2009, Imam Feisal Abdul Rauf proposed building an Islamic community center called Cordoba House (later renamed Park51) in lower Manhattan, a few blocks away from Ground Zero. This space was already in use as a place of worship, but the imam's plan was to build a large community center. Plans for the center, which would be open to Muslims and non-Muslims alike, included recreational facilities (swimming pool, gym, basketball court), an auditorium, a restaurant and culinary school, educational programs and exhibitions, a library and reading room, art studios, childcare services, and a September 11 memorial, in addition to prayer space. One of the goals of the center, besides providing facilities for the community, was to foster relationships and communication between Muslims and non-Muslims. Organizers hoped that these personal interactions and educational programs would build understanding and tolerance in the community.

After the project was approved by the New York City community board on May 6, 2010, blogger Pamela Geller wrote a post about the center on her blog, *Atlas Shrugs*. In "Monster Mosque Pushes Ahead in Shadow of World Trade Center Islamic Death and Destruction," Geller wrote:

The only Muslim center that should be built in the shadow of the World Trade Center is one devoted to expunging the Koran and all Islamic teachings of the prescribed violent jihad and all hateful texts and incitement to violence ... That is the only kind of Islamic center that would be appropriate, though it probably wouldn't last two minutes without being bombed by devout Muslims.

Geller called the center a "victory lap" for the terrorists and claimed that building the center "demonstrates the territorial nature of Islam. This is Islamic domination and expansionism." She referred to the Muslim American community as "a manically sensitive bunch" who "[wail] on us infidels about Muslim sensitivities and anticipatory and imaginary affronts and insults," rejecting the concept of Islamophobia altogether.

An Islamophobic ad sponsored by various organizations in the Islamophobia network appears in the New York City subway on September 27, 2012.

Geller is the executive director of the American Freedom Defense Initiative and the co-founder (with Robert Spencer) of the organization Stop Islamization of America (SIOA). Both organizations have been designated active anti-Muslim hate groups by the Southern Poverty Law Center. Geller's American Freedom Defense Initiative sponsored billboards and ads that were displayed on New York City's MTA buses and subway stations. One placed at the Hartsdale, New York, Metro North train station read, "It's not Islamophobia, It's Islamorealism."

Geller, Spencer, and the SIOA organized a campaign called "Stop the 911 Mosque" and held rallies near the proposed site (one on the anniversary of D-Day and one on the anniversary of the 9/11 attacks). The "Ground Zero Mosque" controversy became a national story, and soon the issue was being debated in the mainstream media and by conservative politicians. Falling as it did around the time of the midterm election campaigns of 2010, the mosque issue was politicized.

Former House Speaker Newt Gingrich stated that "the folks who want to build this mosque—who are really radical Islamists who want to triumphally prove that they can build a mosque right next to a place where three thousand Americans were killed by radical Islamists—those folks don't have any interest in reaching out to the community. They're trying to make a case about supremacy." He also compared it to the Nazis placing a monument next to the Holocaust Museum or the Japanese putting up a site next to Pearl Harbor. Former vice-presidential candidate Sarah Palin stated that "to build a

The Islamophobia Network

People like Pamela Geller, Lou Ann Zelenik, and their organizations are all part of a small but influential group that controls the organized Islamophobia movement. In 2011, the Center for American Progress released a study, *Fear, Inc.*, which demonstrates in detail how a well-funded group of "misinformation experts" spreads Islamophobia to the public through a group of advocates, the media, and grassroots organizations. The study shows that from 2001 to 2009, more than $42 million was donated to organizations that promote Islamophobia. These donations fund think tanks and individual "experts" who publish misinformation in the form of books, videos, blogs, reports, and websites. The mainstream media, politicians, and religious groups then use these published "facts" to mislead the public and create a negative perception of Muslims and Islam.

The network uses two main tactics in order to convince the public that Islam is a threat to America. It argues that the violent jihadists are the Muslims who are properly interpreting the Islamic religious texts and sharia (Islamic religious law), and that other Muslims are misinterpreting their own religion. They also attack and slander moderate Muslim individuals and organizations in America, accusing them of being spies for terrorist organizations bent on destroying the West from the inside.

Some of the main organizations in the network are:
- The Center for Security Policy

- The David Horowitz Freedom Center
- The Society of Americans for National Existence
- The Middle East Forum
- Jihad Watch
- Stop Islamization of America
- The Investigative Project on Terrorism.
- ACT! for America and American Council for Truth.
- The American Freedom Defense Initiative

mosque at Ground Zero is a stab in the heart of the families of the innocent victims of those horrific attacks." The media coverage of the "Ground Zero Mosque" fed the public a lot of misinformation about the nature of the community center and the Muslim community and reinforced the Islamophobic idea of collective responsibility—that all of Islam was to blame for the events of September 11.

The Park51 controversy was the most highly publicized because of the proposed center's proximity to Ground Zero, but there were battles over mosques in other parts of the country as well. In Murfreesboro, Tennessee, a mosque proposed in 2010 met with a great deal of resistance from residents and local politicians. Opponents of the mosque vandalized a sign designating the site of the future Islamic Center of Murfreesboro by spray-painting "Not Welcome" on it, and some construction equipment at the building site was set on fire. Congressional candidate Lou Ann Zelenik issued a statement in which she called the proposed mosque an "Islamic training center" and stated that "until the American Muslim community find it in their hearts to separate themselves from their evil, radical counterparts, to condemn those who want to destroy our civilization and will fight against them, we are not obligated to open our society to any of them." In March 2011, Zelenik founded an anti-Muslim group, the Tennessee Freedom Coalition.

Burning Mad

In 2010, Pastor Terry Jones of Dove World Outreach Center, a Christian church in Gainesville, Florida, sparked an international incident when he planned "International Burn a Koran Day" for the ninth anniversary of the September 11 attacks. The church website said the event was organized "in remembrance

of the fallen victims of 9/11 and to stand against the evil of Islam. Islam is of the devil!" The web page for the event included Photoshopped images that encouraged a nuclear attack on the Grand Mosque in Mecca.

Several high-level US government officials, including

Demonstrators in Tehran, Iran, protest Florida pastor Terry Jones.

President Obama, urged Jones not to go through with the burning as they feared it would endanger American soldiers stationed in Afghanistan and Iraq. Jones ultimately cancelled the 9/11 event but continued to spread his message around the country. On March 20, 2011, Jones held a "mock trial" for the Quran at his church. He acted as judge, and twelve members of his congregation sat on the jury. The jury convicted the Quran of being guilty of "crimes against humanity," including promoting terrorism and "the death, rape and torture of people worldwide whose only crime is not being of the Islamic faith." They then took an online poll in which the majority voted to set the Quran on fire. The burning was recorded and posted on the church's website.

On April 1, 2011, in direct response to Jones's Quran burning, violent protests broke out in Mazar-i-Sharif, Afghanistan, resulting in protestors storming the United Nations building. Seven foreigners and several protestors died in the incident. Another protest in Kandahar left nine people dead and almost one hundred injured. Jones issued a statement in which he said, "We must hold these countries and people accountable for what they have done … Islam is not a religion of peace. It is time that we call these people to accountability."

Islamophobia in Politics

One of the major political players connected to the Islamophobia network is Michele Bachmann, the founder of the Tea Party Caucus and former US congresswoman from Minnesota. Bachmann launched a smear campaign against Muslim American State Department staffer Huma Abedin in which she claimed Abedin had connections to extremist organizations and posed a threat to national security. Bachmann has also stated publicly that Islam is incompatible with the West, called it a "doctrine of demons," and perpetuated the myth that Muslims are trying to take over the West through the implementation of sharia law.

Congressman Peter King of New York, who has served as chairman of the House Subcommittee on Counterterrorism and Intelligence, has a long history of Islamophobia. In a 2004 interview with Sean Hannity, King said that the majority of mosques in America were controlled by Islamic fundamentalists, called American Muslims "an enemy living among us," and falsely claimed that Muslim leaders do not condemn terrorist attacks or cooperate with authorities. At the time of this interview, King was promoting his novel, *Vale of Tears*, a fictional story about a congressman who tries to stop a terrorist attack in New York City. King has also stated that there are too many mosques in America.

As chairman of the House Homeland Security Committee, King held four congressional hearings regarding the radicalization of American Muslims beginning in March 2011. These hearings were highly public and cast suspicion on the entire Muslim community. They did not result in any actual evidence that American Muslims were being radicalized; in fact, 2011 terrorism statistics showed that there were almost twice as many terrorist plots by non-Muslims than there were by Muslims since September 11, 2001.

The Role of the Media

The most watched source of news in America is Fox News Network. Fox's programs often feature Islamophobic terrorism "experts." On America's top-rated news program, *The O'Reilly Factor*, host Bill O'Reilly uses his platform to present his view of Islam to his millions of viewers. On a May 19, 2011 broadcast, O'Reilly said, "For every Muslim in the world that wants democracy and wants human rights, there is one who doesn't. And the one who doesn't, doesn't have any rules. And it will blow the hell out of the one that does." O'Reilly also famously said that "there is a Muslim problem in the world" during a November 23, 2010, interview with Whoopi Goldberg. On October 15, 2010, Fox News Radio host Brian Kilmeade defended O'Reilly's anti-Muslim statements and said, "Not every Muslim is an extremist, a terrorist, but every terrorist is a Muslim."

Bo Dietl, a former New York City police detective who often appears on Fox News, appeared on *Your World* on August 7, 2007, and stated, "We know there's a war by fundamentalists and terrorists to kill us. So we have to be able to profile. And I'm sorry, if I see two guys that look like Aba Daba Doo and Aba Daba Dah, I'm gonna pull 'em over, and I wanna find out what you're doing." This sentiment was echoed by Fox contributor Tom McInerney on the January 2, 2010, edition of *America's News HQ*. McInerney said, "We have to use profiling. And I mean be very serious and harsh about the profiling. If you are an eighteen- to twenty-eight-year-old Muslim man, then you should be strip-searched."

Islamophobia is not limited to conservative pundits. The otherwise liberal Bill Maher, whose HBO show *Real Time with Bill Maher* is popular among liberal and left-leaning viewers, is notoriously critical of organized religion. Maher does not believe that Islamophobia is a real and problematic thing that occurs in society. On the October 2, 2015, show, he said that "Islamophobe" is "a silly word that means nothing." On the same program he said that Islam and Muslims are treated like a "protected species" that can't be criticized or discussed without it being called racist or discriminatory. He has referred to the **burqa**—a full-body garment worn by some Muslim women—as a "beekeeper's suit." Some of his most virulent anti-Muslim commentary occurred on the October 6, 2014, episode, when Maher referred to Islam as the "only religion that acts like the mafia" and will "kill you if you say the wrong thing, draw the wrong picture, or write the wrong book."

Another major source of Islamophobia in the media comes from the Religious Right. The Christian Broadcasting Network (CBN) airs *The 700 Club*, hosted by network founder Pat Robertson. Robertson has a long history of anti-Muslim prejudice. He has compared Muslims to Nazis, called them fanatics, and claimed that Islam teaches violence. On the April 8, 2008, broadcast of *The 700 Club*, Robertson said:

> Islam is not a religion, it is a political system bent on world domination, not a religion. It masquerades as a religion, but the religion covers a worldwide attempt to exercise power and to subjugate the world to their way

of thinking. They want a caliphate as they had once before; they want all people to be subjected to Sharia and to live under their rules and their domination. It is every bit as insidious as Communism, perhaps more so. But to say, "Well, it's a religion, and you should leave a religion alone," that's just not the way it works.

In the same broadcast, he stated that, while Christianity is the way to freedom, Islam is the way to slavery. In 1990, Robertson founded the American Center for Law and Justice (ACLJ). The ACLJ was involved in trying to block the Park51 center and also called for an investigation into the prayer sessions of the Congressional Muslim Staff Association.

In addition to all the Islamophobic rhetoric on the news, the programming also focuses on the spectacle of terrorist attacks. News programs mostly air stories about Muslims who are linked to terrorist activity and ignore the positive contributions of the Muslim community. This reinforces the false idea that "all terrorists are Muslims." It also has the effect of isolating and othering American Muslims because the public is rarely shown everyday Muslims who are fully integrated into American society.

Airport Security and Profiling

The experience of air travel in the United States changed forever after the September 11 attacks. The fact that all nineteen of the 9/11 hijackers were able to pass through security checks in multiple airports led many to question the effectiveness of the current system. The US government federalized airport security under the Aviation and Transportation Security Act, which created the Transportation Security Administration (TSA) within the Department of Homeland Security. Airport security had previously been handled by private companies hired by individual airports. The TSA was created to oversee new security measures implemented in American airports.

Before 9/11, nonticketed passengers were allowed through security. People could drop friends and loved ones off at their gate and watch them board, and they could meet them at their gate when they arrived. In the post-9/11 world, only passengers with tickets may pass through security to the gate area. The tickets are often double- or triple-checked against photo ID before a passenger can even go through the screening area. Passengers are also forced to take off shoes and outer layers of clothing before passing through, and there are ever more complex machines to pass through (including full-body scanners). Severe restrictions have been placed on what kind and how much liquid and liquid-based products (restricted to 3.4 ounces, or 100 milliliters, or less) one can bring onto a plane. In many cases, this means that if people want to bring their own toiletries, they are forced to check their bag instead of using a carry-on. There are also random physical pat-downs by members of the TSA that some people find incredibly intrusive.

The aircraft themselves were fortified, especially the doors, and the law enforcement branch of the TSA—the Federal Air Marshall Service—was expanded. Air marshals are permitted to carry concealed weapons on airplanes and are trained to blend in with the other passengers. Pilots have full authority to remove passengers at their and the flight crew members' discretion.

These airport security measures, while inconvenient for the average traveler, have a much more serious effect on Muslims, Arabs, and Sikhs, who are disproportionately chosen for excessive screening. They are often questioned, removed from planes, and even detained by authorities for no reason other than their physical appearance, their names, or the fact that they speak Arabic. It is not just the airport security personnel who discriminate against these travelers. Both airline employees and other passengers have been known to engage in Islamophobic profiling in airports and on airplanes. The association of the 9/11 hijackers and other terrorists with Islam has been ingrained so deeply into the American consciousness that it elicits an immediate fear and suspicion of innocent passengers—a fear that is based on nothing but guilt by association, whether physical or religious or both.

Mohamed Ahmed Radwan was kicked off an American Airlines flight from Charlotte, North Carolina, to Detroit, Michigan, in December 2015. Radwan later filed a complaint with the help of the Council on American-Islamic Relations (CAIR). The complaint states that a flight attendant used the intercom to announce publicly, "Mohamed Ahmed, Seat 25-A: I will be watching you." She called him out twice more by name and seat number before calling him "too sensitive" and then removing him from the plane because she was "uncomfortable" with him. The complaint noted many other instances of discrimination in air travel. Among them was an incident involving Khairuldeen Makhzoomi, a twenty-six-year-old student at UC Berkeley, who was kicked off a Southwest Airlines flight for speaking Arabic on the phone with his uncle. Makhzoomi was removed from the plane and held for questioning by police and the FBI. He was searched, and authorities brought in bomb-sniffing police dogs. He was completely innocent and Southwest later refunded his ticket, but the airline insisted that they had followed standard procedure.

In January 2016, four Brooklyn men—three Muslim and one Sikh—were removed from a plane because the flight attendants and pilot were uncomfortable with them. The men were part of a group of friends traveling home after a short vacation together in Montreal. They switched their travel plans at the last minute to fly together, and two of the men decided to upgrade to business class; another two switched seats with other passengers to sit next to each other on the way home. This was enough to get them kicked off the plane and detained. They filed a multimillion-dollar discrimination lawsuit against American Airlines.

On March 26, 2016, Eaman-Amy Saad Shebley was kicked off a United Airlines flight with her husband and three children. She said the incident began after she had asked a flight attendant a question about the harness for her child's safety seat. She posted video of the interaction in a shareable Facebook post that says, "Shame on you #unitedAirlines for profiling my family and me for no reason other than how we look." The pilot gives no concrete reason why they are being kicked off; he says only that it is his decision and that the family is being removed because of a "safety flight issue."

Bullying and Discrimination in Schools

Bias-based bullying of Muslim and Arab students is on the rise in American schools. A CAIR study reports that around 50 percent of Muslim students have been bullied even though there are antibullying laws in most states. Students and teachers have been guilty of discriminating against and bullying Muslim and Arab students. Bullying has been designated a public health issue in American schools and has wide-ranging negative effects on children and young adults. Some of the worst effects of bullying include fear of going to school, increased rates of truancy, reduced concentration,

Muslim students at Fordson High School in Dearborn, Michigan, eat lunch with non-Muslim peers on "Mix It Up Day."

poor grades, sleep disturbances, high levels of depression and/or anxiety, loneliness, low self-esteem, and fear for personal safety.

American public school populations are becoming more and more diverse, yet the standard curriculum is still focused on white European and American history, art, literature, and achievements. Ethnic studies, especially of the Middle East, are often ignored completely or are relegated to specially designated days, months, or otherwise marginal positions within the curriculum. When there is educational material related to Muslim and Arabic culture, it can spark controversy among parents and members of the community with anti-Muslim biases.

In December 2015, the schools in Augusta County, Virginia, were shut down due to a large volume of complaints and threats received in response to a homework assignment. The World Geography curriculum's unit on world religions included a section on Arabic calligraphy in a homework assignment, and students were asked to try to copy the calligraphy of the *shahada*, or Islamic statement of faith: "There is no god but Allah, and Muhammad is the messenger of Allah." The shahada was not translated, nor were students asked to translate or recite the statement. The goal of the exercise was simply for students to appreciate the beauty of Arabic calligraphy.

Still, many parents were outraged and believed that the assignment was a form of indoctrination. They called for the school to fire the teacher even though she was using an approved workbook that the school had been using for many years. People sent hateful and profane emails to the school district, including pictures of beheadings. One mother of a nine-year-old student in the district stated, "The sheet [the teacher] gave out was pure doctrine in its origin ... I will not have my children sit under a woman who indoctrinates them with the Islam religion when I am a Christian."

All across the country, national anti-Muslim groups such as ACT! for America and the American Center for Law and Justice have argued against the inclusion of Islam and Islamic world history in public school curriculums. They believe that it is not education but indoctrination.

It is not uncommon for female Muslim students who wear the traditional **hijab** to be assaulted when bullies taunt them and physically remove their headscarves against their will. Muslim students are called a variety of ethnic slurs, branded "terrorist" or "ISIS," and are often the subject of jokes about bombings or other violent attacks. Like other forms of bullying, this is exacerbated by social media. A single post branding someone a terrorist can spread to the entire school (and beyond) within minutes, and the post is often impossible to remove from the internet after it has spread. Silence on the part of teachers and faculty is also part of the problem when it comes to bias-based bullying of Muslim and Arab students. Some schools offer cultural sensitivity training for faculty, but more often teachers are left on their own to deal with Islamophobic bullying and are not equipped to handle the subject.

Job Discrimination

Even though the United States has laws in place to protect citizens' religious freedom, Muslims are routinely persecuted and discriminated against in the workplace because of their faith. They are often denied the religious accommodations they need to freely practice their religion, and this is especially true for women who choose to wear traditional dress. In August 2016, George Mason University student Najaf Khan was forced to choose between wearing her hijab and keeping her job as a dental assistant at Fair Oaks Dental Care in Fairfax,

A Florida gun store declares itself a Muslim-free zone and refuses services to Muslim Americans.

Virginia. Her boss told her he wanted to keep religion out of the office and that her headscarf would "offend patients." Her boss gave her an ultimatum: keep it on and lose your job or take it off and stay. Khan said she would not compromise her religion, at which point the boss held the door open for her and she left. Khan reached out to the Council on American Islamic Relations for help. CAIR issued the following statement: "No employee should face termination because of his or her faith or religious practices. We call on Fair Oaks Dental Care to reinstate the Muslim employee and to offer her reasonable religious accommodation as mandated by law."

Some businesses go as far as to ban Muslim customers, especially gun stores and shooting ranges. There is a wave of faith-based discrimination at gun stores across the country. They refuse to sell guns to Muslims and put up signs at their businesses making it clear that Muslims are not welcome, both at the store and in the community that supports it. Americans often invoke the Second Amendment right to bear arms as one of the most cherished constitutional rights, yet Muslim Americans are being denied that right because of their religious affiliation. A wave of business discrimination took place after a mass shooting in Chattanooga, Tennessee, in July 2015. The shooter, Mohammad Abdulazeez, fired on a military recruiting center and a navy operations support center, killing four marines and a sailor. As is so often the case when a shooter is Muslim, the rest of the Muslim and Arab American communities suffered the consequences of Abdulazeez's actions.

FOUR

Combating Islamophobia

The Islamophobia network has a lot of money and a lot of power, and their voices are very loud, but there are many members of the Muslim American and Arab American communities who work tirelessly to thwart their efforts. From national organizations, to interfaith coalitions, to grassroots groups, to individual people making an effort to learn, there are plenty of ways to combat Islamophobia in the United States in the face of so much hate.

Council on American-Islamic Relations

Established in 1994, the Council on American-Islamic Relations (CAIR) is a grassroots civil rights and advocacy group that works to enhance understanding of Islam, encourage dialogue, protect civil liberties, empower American Muslims, and build coalitions that promote justice and mutual understanding. It is

Opposite: Supporters of the Park51 Islamic community center rally in lower Manhattan on September 11, 2010.

The "Islamophobin" Campaign

In May 2016, CAIR launched a satirical social media campaign to promote awareness of the growing problem of Islamophobia in America. They made a mock TV commercial for a new "drug" to cure Islamophobia. The product (which is actually just sugar-free gum) is called Islamophobin and is designed to look like an over-the-counter medicine. The box reads: "Multi-Symptom Relief for Chronic Islamophobia. Maximum Strength Formula Treats Blind Intolerance, Unthinking Bigotry, Irrational Fear of Muslims, and U.S. Presidential Election Year Scapegoating. Take two and call a Muslim in the morning. Warning: May result in peaceful coexistence." The website for the product, which is available for purchase, states: "ISLAMOPHOBIN® is right for you if you: Fear and hate Muslims; Are suspicious of people who don't look like you, sound like you, dress like you, or believe as you; Get abnormally nervous when you see a Muslim or someone who you think is Muslim; Pray that a Muslim is not on your flight."

An activist from the group CodePink hands out fake pills called "Islamophobin" created by CAIR in an effort to fight Islamophobia.

CAIR handed out packets of Islamophobin at an anti-Trump rally on the first day of the 2016 Republican National Convention in Cleveland, Ohio. On a more serious note, it also held a press conference during which CAIR's executive director, Nihad Awad, spoke about the dangerous Islamophobic rhetoric and general hostility toward minority groups displayed by the then presumptive nominee Donald Trump.

most Muslims as Arab). The truth is that the Arab American community is an incredibly diverse mix of religious and cultural traditions. The Arab American Institute Foundation's stated goal is "to encourage, recognize, and celebrate Arab American participation in American civic life, and to cultivate and mobilize a strong, educated, empowered Arab American community that can play a meaningful role in the betterment of our country."

The foundation sponsors outreach programs that help educate the public, government agencies, and organizations about the contributions and concerns of Arab Americans. Outreach efforts include educational presentations to both non-Arab Americans and Arab visitors about the Arab American identity, as well as the community's contributions in the realms of American civic life, government, business, and education. The hope is that education and personal interaction will foster more positive interactions between Arab Americans and non-Arab Americans, especially members of law enforcement.

Part of being a good American citizen is having a sense of responsibility to one's community and giving back when you can. The Arab American Institute Foundation is very dedicated to this type of public service. Their annual Arab American Service Day is a way to highlight the community's dedication to American civic life as well as perform necessary tasks to give back to communities in need. Past service projects include building houses, serving food, and creating sustainable community gardens. In this way, the foundation hopes to foster goodwill and demonstrate that Arab Americans are just as invested in American civic life as anyone else.

The Arab American Institute (AAI) is slightly different than the foundation in that it is focused specifically on Arab American political participation. The institute has two main areas of focus: campaigns and elections, and policy formation and research. The AAI serves as a resource to government officials, the media, political leaders, and community groups on a variety of public policy issues concerning Arab Americans and US-Arab relations.

Interfaith Efforts

Solidarity between members of different religious communities is essential to stemming the tide of Islamophobia in America and around the globe. Interfaith dialogue is crucial to fostering understanding and constructive conversations between people of different faiths. Religious leaders have a lot of influence within their individual communities, and when they stand together with Muslims, they are better able to preach religious tolerance to their congregations.

One such organization is Shoulder-to-Shoulder, a coalition of thirty-two religious denominations and organizations. It was founded in 2010 in response to the Park51 controversy and the planned Quran burnings on the ninth anniversary of September 11. More than forty religious leaders held an interfaith press conference in Washington, DC, on September 7, 2010. In the statement, they urged spiritual leaders across America to "denounce categorically derision, misinformation or outright bigotry directed against any religious group in this country. Silence is not an option. Only by taking this stand, can spiritual leaders fulfill the highest calling of our respective faiths, and thereby help to create a safer and stronger America for all of our people."

Shoulder-to-Shoulder's motto is "Standing with American Muslims; Upholding American Values," and to do this they work at all levels—from grassroots organizing to meetings with Congress and the White House. They organize seminars and webinars as well as provide research and educational material in order to bring people of all faiths together in solidarity with the Muslim American community.

Muslims in Congress

The first Muslim elected to the United States Congress is Keith Ellison (D-MN). He took office in 2007 and was sworn in using Thomas Jefferson's copy of the Quran. His choice to use the Quran outraged conservative columnist and talk radio host Dennis Prager. Prager wrote a viciously Islamophobic piece called, "America, Not Keith Ellison, Decides What Book a Congressman Takes His Oath On," in which he opined that Ellison's decision to use the Quran would "embolden Islamic extremists and make new ones" and that terrorists would see

Minnesota Democrat Keith Ellison is sworn in using the Quran on January 4, 2007.

it as "the first sign of the realization of their greatest goal—the Islamicization of America." In the same piece, he stated that the Bible was the only acceptable book for an American to use while swearing in. He then compared the Quran to "the Nazi's bible," Hitler's *Mein Kampf*—something echoed by Sean Hannity on Fox News.

Congressman Virgil Goode (R-VA) used the Ellison Quran controversy to further his anti-immigrant agenda, despite the fact that Ellison was born Detroit, Michigan. Goode expressed fear of a Muslim immigrant takeover of America and urged voters to "adopt the strict immigration policies that I believe are necessary to preserve the values and beliefs traditional to the United States of America."

Ellison has been scrutinized and attacked by some in the media because of his faith. He has been accused of having terrorist ties and infiltrating the US government to promote sharia law from the inside. He was also accused of being anti-Semitic because of his association with the Nation of Islam in the 1990s. Ellison has since stated that at that time he had not "adequately scrutinized the positions and statements" of Louis Farrakhan and the NOI and has fully rejected the Nation of Islam.

In 2008, Ellison was joined in Congress by another Muslim, André Carson (D-IN). His time in office has been no easier than Ellison's and has included a death threat that was called into his Washington office in December 2015. Despite their hardships, Ellison and Carson have many supporters, and they will continue to speak out against bigotry and work within the government to fix America's Islamophobia problem from the top down.

Muslim Charity Work

Much gets made of jihad and the threat of a sharia theocracy coming to America, but not nearly enough is said about zakat: the third of the five pillars of Islam. In the wake of attacks, the Muslim community routinely comes together to help with recovery efforts. Muslims believe that charity toward others is required of all people who are physically and financially able to do so.

Immediately after 9/11, national Muslim organizations like CAIR and the Muslim Public Affairs Council (MPAC) issued statements condemning the attacks but also calling on the Muslim community to provide whatever help they can to victims and families. Muslim relief agencies organized

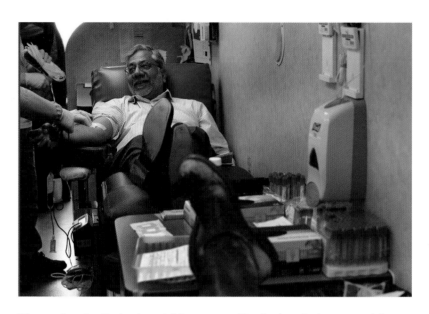

Waseem Sayed, a Muslim from California, gives blood to benefit the victims of the April 2013 Boston Marathon bombing.

to support recovery efforts, and individual Muslim citizens donated blood and financial aid to relief agencies working at the scene.

In the wake of the Boston Marathon bombing, CAIR directed people to give blood to the Red Cross and also made it a point to direct any witnesses at the marathon to contact law enforcement. They noted that while thoughts and prayers "can serve as comfort to those in physical and emotional pain," it is also necessary to take tangible action. Generic "thoughts and prayers" tweets from most politicians, public figures, and celebrities included no such call to action but received a lot of publicity online and in the media. This only serves to reinforcing a stereotypical portrayal of Muslims.

Making a Change

A great deal of focus is placed on what Muslims can do to fight Islamophobia and not enough on what the average American citizen can do to promote religious tolerance and awareness. Education and communication are the most important tools we can use to fight prejudice. The first thing to do is to learn about Islam, Muslim Americans, and the Arab American community and to share that knowledge with others. Follow civil rights groups on social media to keep up to date on the news and events. Share articles and posts about Islamophobia with your friends and family—it's an easy and effective way to amplify the voices of the victims. Attend a community event at a local mosque and meet some new people—there is no weapon stronger than open and constructive conversation.

Part of being a good citizen is participating in the political process, so make sure to find out who represents you in Congress and urge them to support anti-Muslim bigotry legislation, if they haven't already done so. Support businesses that speak out against Islamophobia and boycott ones that discriminate. Volunteer with a civil rights organization or charity that focuses on anti-Muslim, anti-Arab, and/or anti-immigrant bigotry. Finally, always report any Islamophobic hate crimes you witness to the local police and/or the FBI—the "if you see something, say something" thing goes both ways. Do not sit idly by while innocent people are being victimized. Speak up.

FIVE

Rising Rhetoric

Terrorist attacks at home and abroad plus the continued atrocities committed in the Middle East and around the world have made for fertile ground in growing Islamophobia. They may have even impacted the 2016 presidential campaign.

Republican candidate Donald Trump took advantage of a series of terrorist attacks that began in 2015 to gain support from the electorate. "Trumpism" has four characteristics as defined by *The Hill*, a politics blog. These include celebrity, nativism, populism, and being a Washington outsider. Nativism brings with it intense xenophobia, **white nationalism**, and racism. Trump's personal attacks on members of the media and other statements opened him up to charges of misogyny. Being an outsider portrayed Trump "as the savior of the disenfranchised," wrote David Edward Tabachnick on the blog.

Nativism has been present in American politics in other election cycles. In the late 1840s, the arrival of many

Opposite: New York City's iconic Washington Square Arch is lit in the colors of the French flag after the November 15, 2015, terrorist attacks in Paris.

immigrants from Ireland and Germany sparked anti-Catholic sentiment and fears over job loss to the new arrivals. These fears grew into a political party.

The American Party grew in the 1850s and it became known as the Know Nothing Party. The name is based on the fact that early supporters were told to say they know nothing when they were asked about nativist organizations to which they belonged. As the organizations gained support, its members could be more open about their beliefs, and the party grew in popularity. It called for immigration restrictions, a twenty-one-year wait for immigrants to become citizens (the current wait is five years), and a ban on voting or on holding a public office for anyone not born in the United States.

At its peak in 1855, the American Party held forty-three seats in Congress. However, in the 1856 election, Millard Fillmore, the party's nominee for president, won only the state of Maryland. The party then split over the issue of slavery and fell apart.

Immigration also was an issue in American politics at the turn of the twentieth century, when nativists wanted to restrict or exclude Asians from the United States. Political pressure after the Japanese attack on Pearl Harbor led to the internment of more than one hundred thousand people of Japanese descent who were living on the West Coast. Many of these people were American citizens. The loss of civil rights by Japanese Americans is a dark stain in our country's history.

Tensions between various cultural groups are on the rise as the face of America becomes more racially, ethnically, and religiously diverse. US involvement in the Middle East and North Africa and the increased terrorist activity of ISIS are of great concern to the American people. Statements by Trump such as "Islam hates us" have incited fear, prejudice, and violence in the United States. Islamophobia in America is worse than ever.

Paris Attacks

On November 13, 2015, a group of nine ISIS terrorists carried out a series of coordinated attacks across Paris, France. These gunmen and suicide bombers targeted various high-traffic areas around the city: a stadium during a soccer game, the Bataclan Theater during a concert, and restaurants and bars packed with Friday night crowds. The attacks, which left 130 dead and hundreds injured, were the deadliest on French soil since World War II. All of the ISIS terrorists were citizens of the European Union who had been radicalized in Syria. They were on the terrorist watch list, but they took advantage of the Syrian refugee crisis to get back into the EU. ISIS claimed responsibility for the attacks, saying they were retaliation for France bombing ISIS locations in Syria and Iraq.

There was an international outpouring of support. Much like after 9/11, the global community came together in support of France. Iconic buildings and landmarks across the world lit up in the colors of the French flag, people held vigils outside of French embassies around the world, and world leaders pledged their solidarity with France. As so often happens, along with the grief and sympathy came a backlash against Muslims both abroad and at home. A new wave of Islamophobia in America began in earnest after the Paris attacks despite the fact that, as they always do, the nation's major Islamic groups all condemned ISIS and the attacks. Regardless, there was a wave of violent attacks on mosques and individuals perceived as Muslim, and an increase of anti-Muslim bias and rhetoric in the media and on the internet. Politicians used the opportunity to push their anti-immigrant and anti-Muslim agendas.

The evening of the attacks, Senator Ted Cruz (R-TX)—then a Republican presidential candidate—proposed that the United States immediately halt the immigration of any Syrian war refugees. He also stated: "We must immediately recognize that our enemy is not 'violent extremism.' It is the radical Islamism that has declared jihad against the West. It will not be appeased by outreach or declarations of tolerance." A few days later, Cruz revised his remarks, saying that he would allow Christian Syrians into America because "there

Canadians rally in Toronto on November 22, 2015, in support of Prime Minister Justin Trudeau's pledge to admit twenty-five thousand Syrian refugees into Canada by the end of 2015.

is no meaningful risk of Christians committing acts of terror. If there were a group of radical Christians pledging to murder anyone who had a different religious view than they, we would have a different national security situation."

Such statements ignore the fact that, according to FBI statistics, non-Muslims are responsible for the majority of terrorist violence in the United States. Not only that, but Christian terrorists exist in America and they have for a very long time. The history of the Ku Klux Klan alone is enough to demonstrate that terrorist violence is not solely an Islamic problem. Just as not all Protestant Christians are members of the KKK, not all Muslims are members of ISIS. Throughout history, extremists of every major world religion have twisted their religious writings and used their faith to justify acts of violence.

Homegrown Extremists

Things went from bad to worse in America on December 2, 2015, when a husband and wife—Syed Rizwan Farook and Tashfeen Malik—carried out a premeditated terrorist attack in San Bernardino, California. Farook was born in America to Pakistani immigrant parents; Malik was born in Pakistan and legally immigrated to the United States. The couple targeted a staff meeting/holiday party of the San Bernardino County health department where Farook worked. The couple used AR-15 automatic rifles (their homemade bombs did not explode) to kill fourteen people and injure twenty-one others. Both were killed in a shootout with the police after the attacks. Investigators later discovered that the couple had been radicalized and were planning the attacks

Je Suis Charlie

The November 2015 ISIS attacks came only ten months after a mass shooting at the *Charlie Hebdo* newspaper offices in Paris. *Charlie Hebdo* is a satirical French weekly that had a history of publishing highly controversial cartoons of Muhammad that offended many Muslims. In the past, cartoonist Stéphane Charbonnier ("Charb") and the rest of *Charlie Hebdo* had received threats. The office was firebombed, and its website was hacked by extremists from al-Qaeda in Yemen, who believed that it was blasphemous to visually depict Muhammad. The two men who attacked the paper used automatic weapons to kill twelve people, including Charbonnier, and injure eleven others.

The international community came together to condemn these attacks as a violation of free speech and freedom of the press. *Je Suis Charlie* ("I Am Charlie") was adopted as the slogan of solidarity, and it was a trending hashtag on Twitter. Citizens around the globe, including world leaders and Hollywood stars, tweeted #JeSuisCharlie in addition to their sympathies. The phrase even made its way onto the red carpet at the Golden Globes on January 11. Human rights attorney Amal Clooney wore a "Je Suis Charlie" pin on her purse, and a number of other celebrities held up signs.

Amal Clooney wears a *Je Suis Charlie* pin on her purse at the Golden Globes.

for some time. On December 5, ISIS claimed responsibility for the attacks and referred to Farook and Malik as followers of the Islamic State. While the couple may have been ISIS-inspired, there is no direct link between the homegrown extremists and ISIS nor any evidence that they belonged to any terrorist cell in the United States.

The San Bernardino slaughter was followed not long after by the worst terrorist attack on American soil since 9/11. At 2 a.m. on June 12, 2016, Omar Mateen entered Pulse, a gay nightclub in Orlando, Florida, and committed the deadliest mass shooting in US history. It was Latin Night at the club, and most of the forty-nine people killed were members of the Latinx LGBT community, making the Orlando shooting the deadliest attack ever to target the American LGBT community. Mateen was born in New York State to Afghan parents. He pledged his allegiance to ISIS during a 911 call made from inside Pulse and said the attack was retaliation for US bombings in Syria and Iraq. Mateen expressed solidarity with the Tsarnaev brothers and Moner Abu-Salha, the first American suicide bomber in Syria. He was shot and killed by police after a three-hour-long standoff.

The reactions after these attacks were predictable: a wave of Islamophobic attacks on individuals perceived to be Muslim and increased Islamophobic rhetoric in the media. As with every terrorist attack that happens at home and abroad, there was heightened fear and anxiety within the American Muslim community. Both Muslim organizations and individuals openly condemned the attacks because it was expected of them, despite their having zero culpability or links to the terrorists.

A memorial stands outside of Pulse nightclub in Orlando, Florida, after the worst mass shooting in American history.

Trump's Muslim Ban

After the Paris attacks, Donald Trump made several comments that added fuel to the fire of anti-Muslim, anti-Arab bias in America. He perpetuated the rumor that thousands of Muslims across the Hudson from New York, in Jersey City, New Jersey, were cheering on 9/11, saying he saw it on television: "There were people over in New Jersey that were watching it, a heavy Arab population, that were cheering as the buildings came down." Trump claimed he had seen these 9/11 celebrations even though the police said that they never happened.

Trump had already said he would not allow Syrian war refugees into the United States, but after the Paris attacks he really kicked up the anti-immigrant rhetoric. He claimed that President Obama was going to let 250,000 refugees into the United States in 2016 when the estimated number of immigrants was actually 10,000. He also claimed that the United States does not screen immigrants properly even though the screening process is extensive and can take almost two years. Trump told NBC News: "We don't know where they're coming from. We don't know who they are. They could be ISIS. It could be the great Trojan horse." It was at this time that he said that as president he would increase surveillance and shut down some American mosques.

Syrian refugees got caught in a game of political football as the number of immigrants who reached the United States by the spring of 2016 lagged behind goals set by the Obama administration. The White House said it would increase efforts to bring in ten thousand refuges without reducing the screening of people seeking asylum in the United States. When the number of refugees increased in June, the administration was accused of cutting corners in the vetting process.

After the San Bernardino attacks, Trump's campaign put out a statement that said, "Donald J. Trump is calling for a total and complete shutdown of Muslims entering the United States until our country's representatives can figure out what is going on." The statement then quoted Trump as saying, "Until we are able to determine and understand this problem and the dangerous threat it poses, our country cannot be the victims of horrendous attacks by people that believe only in Jihad, and have no sense of reason or respect for human life."

Hate Speech and Violence at Trump Rallies

There was an epidemic of hate speech and violence in and around Trump rallies throughout his campaign. This in turn sparked anti-Trump events, some of them at those same rallies. In one case, protestors wanted to keep the candidate from even speaking. A March 11, 2016, rally at the University of Illinois at Chicago had to be canceled because of clashes between Trump supporters and a coalition of UIC student protestors. Students from the Muslim Students Association, the Black Student Union, and the Fearless Undocumented Alliance organized a protest of the Trump rally being held at their school because they felt it posed a safety risk to Muslim, black, and immigrant students. They also did not believe that Trump's message was in keeping with the university's environment of inclusion.

In January 2016, a Muslim woman named Rose Hamid was kicked out of a Trump rally in Rock Hill, South Carolina. She was standing silently, wearing a T-shirt that said "Salam I Come in Peace" and a gold Star of David badge that said "Muslim." This badge was a reference to the ones the Nazis made the Jews wear and was meant as a statement of protest

Police in Cleveland, Ohio, stand guard in Public Square, where anti-Muslim protestors gathered during the 2016 Republican National Convention.

against Trump's comments that he would support a database and religious identification cards for Muslims in America. Hamid told CNN that she was at the rally in order to have personal interactions with Trump supporters and show them that Muslims are just like any other Americans and should not be feared.

There were many other reported incidents at which people at Trump rallies showed their antipathy toward Muslims. One man, who was removed from a rally for refusing to take off a profane T-shirt, told a freelance journalist that the right to free speech entitled him to wear the offending clothing. He said, "You can't make America great again without the First Amendment."

The First Amendment to the Constitution reads: "Congress shall make no law respecting an establishment of religion, or prohibiting the free exercise thereof; or abridging the freedom of speech, or of the press; or the right of the people peaceably to assemble, and to petition the government for a redress of grievances." This amendment protects the right of everyone to express themselves and practice their religion freely, including Muslims.

The Republican National Convention

Intended or not, Donald Trump became a lightning rod for the debate over immigrants by the time he was selected as the Republican nominee for president on July 19, 2016. The Republican National Convention was held in Cleveland, Ohio, and with the delegates came protestors, both pro- and anti-Trump. Outside of Quicken Loans Arena, where the four-night convention took place, anti-Muslim protestors marched down Euclid Street with a police escort. People sported anti-Muslim T-shirts and signs. One man wore a shirt that said, "Allah Is Satan," while another wore one that read "Proud To Be An Infidel." The signs were even more aggressive. One read, "Every Real Muslim is a Jihadist," and another referred to Muhammad as a liar, a false prophet, a pedophile, and a rapist. There was a strong police presence in Cleveland to keep the peace, and protests on both sides were mostly nonviolent.

Inside the arena, the rhetoric coming from the stage was no less aggressive. Newt Gingrich gave a particularly inflammatory speech on July 20 in which he declared, "We are at war with radical Islamists. They are determined to kill us."

Gingrich went on to add the usual postscript—that "the vast majority of Muslims are peaceful"—but made sure to note that even a small percentage of extremists are capable of doing a great deal of damage to America.

Khizr and Ghazala Khan

On July 28, the final day of the Democratic National Convention, two Muslim Americans—Khizr and Ghazala Khan—took the stage in prime time. The Khans lost their son, US Army Captain Humayun Khan, in 2004. Captain Khan was killed in a suicide car bombing in Iraq during Operation Iraqi Freedom. He died protecting his fellow soldiers and local Iraqi citizens and was posthumously awarded a Bronze Star and a Purple Heart. However, as Khizr Khan pointed

Muslims Khizr and Ghazala Khan, the parents of fallen US soldier Humayan Khan, appear at the Democratic National Convention in Philadelphia.

out during his speech, if Donald Trump had been in charge, Humayun would never have been there to save those people.

The Khans are Pakistani immigrants who became United States citizens in 1986. They are what is known as a "Gold Star family"—people who lost an immediate family member in service to the US Armed Forces. Khizr spoke on behalf of his family and had very strong words for Donald Trump:

> Let me ask you: Have you even read the US Constitution? I will gladly lend you my copy. In this document, look for the words "liberty" and "equal protection of law." Have you ever been to Arlington Cemetery? Go look at the graves of the brave patriots who died defending America—you will see all faiths, genders, and ethnicities. You have sacrificed nothing and no one.

During his speech, Khan—a Harvard-educated lawyer—pulled out the pocket Constitution that he always carries with him and held it up as he spoke.

By late summer of 2016, America got a grim reminder of how split the nation is over the topic of Islamophobia. In the New York borough of Queens, an imam and his assistant were shot in the back of the head as they walked home from Saturday prayers. The killings were done execution-style. The imam who died was well respected and was not suspected of extremism. The *New York Daily News* quoted one resident as blaming Trump for the murder because his "drama has created Islamophobia." However, witnesses said the assailant appeared to be Hispanic, an unlikely Trump supporter, and police said the motive could have been robbery. Regardless of motive, this incident illustrates the great distrust between Muslim immigrants and populations with a longer history of residence in the United States.

Persecution Persists

The United States is based on principles that it has often failed to live up to. In the course of the nation's history, Catholics, Jews, Mormons, African Americans, Japanese and other Asian Americans, and women have been subject to the kind of prejudice and hate that Muslim and Arab Americans are currently facing. For a lot of Americans, these things are best left in the past—unfortunate incidents that happened because "things were different back then." But people in those persecuted groups still carry the scars from those wounds. That discrimination and violence has become a part of their cultural experience, and some of it persists to this day in different forms. Today, the increase in Islamophobic hate and violence in America is creating fresh wounds. With the myth of a post-racial, pluralistic America debunked by recent events, more and more Americans are asking: Are things really so different today than they were back then?

America is at a crossroads. In order to put an end to discrimination and religious persecution, the American people need to start embracing the fact that the country is more diverse and multicultural than it once was, and getting more so every day. A diverse population isn't something bad or scary—it's what America has always been and was always supposed to be. Bury the idea that Muslims and immigrants are somehow un-American just because they look different, practice a different religion, or have different cultural practices. Also realize that Muslims, like Christians and Jews, come from many nations. No one group of people gets to define what America is or isn't.

To be American is not to look a certain way, practice a specific faith, or do stereotypically American things; it is to believe in and strive for a democratic society in which all people truly are equal and free. Let this be true for all faiths, all ethnicities, and all immigrants, because when even one American is denied his or her fundamental rights, it undermines the rights of the rest of the citizenry. In the words of Khizr Khan, "We can't solve our problems by building walls and sowing division. We are stronger together." If innocent Muslim citizens are stripped of their rights and freedoms, who will be next?

Major Events in the Growth of Islamophobia

1890–1920: First wave of Arab immigration reaches America.

February 5, 1917: Asiatic Barred Zone Act passed.

May 19, 1921: Emergency Quota Act signed and enacted.

May 26, 1924: Johnson-Reed Act passed.

1929: First mosque in American built in Ross, North Dakota, by Lebanese immigrants.

July 4, 1930: Wallace D. Fard founds the Nation of Islam (NOI) in Detroit, Michigan.

1950s–1960s: Second wave of Arab immigration to America.

July 27, 1952: Immigration and Nationality Act enacted.

June 28, 1957: Islamic Center of Washington dedicated by President Dwight D. Eisenhower.

1965–present: Third wave of Arab immigration to America.

October 3, 1965: Hart-Cellar Act passed.

June 5–10, 1967: Arab-Israeli War, also known as the Six-Day War, is fought.

September 5–6, 1972: Palestinian terrorists take Israeli hostages at the Munich Olympic Games.

April 1, 1979: Iranian Revolution topples the monarchy.

November 4, 1979–January 20, 1981: Iranian Hostage Crisis.

1979-1989: Soviet-Afghan War.

1980: Arab American senator James Abourek founds American-Arab Anti-Discrimination Committee (ADC)

October 11, 1985: ADC office bombed, killing Alex Odeh.

1988: Osama bin Laden founds al-Qaeda

April 23, 1990: President George H. W. Bush, who calls for an end to hate crimes against Muslims and Arabs, signs Hate Crimes Statistics Act.

August 2, 1990–February 28, 1991: Persian Gulf War.

February 26, 1993: World Trade Center bombed.

August 1994: Council on American-Islamic Relations (CAIR) is founded.

April 19, 1995: Alfred P. Murrah Federal Building in Oklahoma City, Oklahoma, is bombed, killing 168.

April 24, 1996: Omnibus Counterterrorism Act signed by President Clinton.

1996: Bin Laden moves al-Qaeda to Afghanistan under Taliban protection; bin Laden issues first fatwa against the United States.

August 7, 1998: Al-Qaeda bombs US embassies in Nairobi, Kenya, and Dar es Salaam, Tanzania.

October 12, 2000: Al-Qaeda bombs the USS *Cole* off the coast of Yemen.

September 11, 2001: Terrorist attacks on New York City; Washington, DC; and Pennsylvania kill about three thousand people.

October 25, 2001: The USA PATRIOT Act is passed.

November 19, 2001: Transportation Security Administration (TSA) is created.

November 25, 2002: Homeland Security Act enacted and national terror threat level advisory system implemented.

March 20, 2003: US goes to war with Iraq.

November 8, 2006: Keith Ellison becomes first Muslim elected to Congress.

November 5, 2009: Fort Hood shootings.

March 9, 2011: Congressman Peter King holds congressional hearings on the radicalization of American Muslims.

April 19, 2013: Boston Marathon bombing.

June 4–10, 2014: ISIS captures Mosul, Iraq, and declares itself a caliphate in Syria and Iraq and demands all Muslims pledge allegiance.

January 7, 2015: *Charlie Hebdo* newspaper office attacked.

November 13, 2015: Terrorists coordinate attacks in Paris, killing 130.

December 2, 2015: A husband and wife of Pakistani ancestry kill fourteen in San Bernardino, California.

June 12, 2016: Omar Mateen kills forty-nine and wounds fifty-three in an attack on an Orlando nightclub.

July 14, 2016: Tunisian Mohamed Lahouaiej Bouhlel drives his truck into a crowd in Nice, France, killing 84 and injuring 202.

GLOSSARY

burqa A long, loose, body-covering garment with veiled holes for the eyes, worn by some Muslim women.

Ground Zero The spot in Manhattan once occupied by the Twin Towers of the World Trade Center. The towers collapsed in the terrorist attacks of September 11, 2001.

hijab A veil covering the head and neck worn in public by some Muslim women.

Islamophobia An exaggerated fear, hatred, and hostility toward Islam and Muslims that is perpetuated by negative stereotypes resulting in bias, discrimination, and the marginalization and exclusion of Muslims from America's social, political, and civil life.

isolationism The policy or doctrine of isolating one's country from the affairs of other nations.

jihad Religious duty to maintain the Islamic faith that includes both an inner spiritual struggle (the "greater jihad") and an outer physical struggle against the enemies of Islam (the "lesser jihad") which may take a violent or nonviolent form.

monolithic Constituting or acting as a single, often rigid, uniform whole.

mosque crawlers NYPD informants who monitored and gathered evidence in the Muslim community, especially in places of worship.

mujahideen Guerrilla fighters engaged in violent jihad, especially those fighting against non-Muslim forces.

nativism A policy of protecting the interests of native-born citizens against those of immigrants.

othering Viewing or treating a person or group of people as intrinsically different from and alien to oneself.

pogrom An organized massacre, especially that of Jews in Russia or eastern Europe.

power vacuum A situation when a country or region has no identifiable central governmental authority.

proxy war A war instigated by a major power in which it does not itself become involved.

rakers Undercover NYPD detectives of the Demographics Unit that spied on local Muslim and Arab communities.

Salafi A fundamentalist who wants to return to the original ways of Islam. It comes from a word that refers to the first three generations of Muslims, starting with those who were companions of Muhammad.

shahada The Islamic profession of faith.

sharia Islamic religious law derived from the Quran and from the teachings and example of the prophet Mohammed.

think tank An institute, corporation, or group organized for interdisciplinary research.

white nationalism An ideology that advocates a racial definition of national identity, especially as promoted by militant white supremacists. This ideology has been used to discriminate against many immigrant groups, including those from China and Japan in the early twentieth century.

xenophobia Intense or irrational dislike, fear, and/or hatred of people from other countries.

zakat The obligatory contribution, similar to a tithe, of a certain portion of one's wealth in support of the poor or needy or for other charitable purposes; third Pillar of Islam.

Books

Bakalian, Anny, and Medhi Bozorgmehr. *Backlash 9/11: Middle Eastern and Muslim Americans Respond.* Berkeley, CA: University of California Press, 2009.

Green, Todd H. *The Fear of Islam: An Introduction to Islamophobia in the West.* Minneapolis, MN: Fortress Press, 2015.

Kayyali, Randa A. *The Arab Americans.* Westport, CT: Greenwood Press, 2006.

Michigan State School of Journalism. *100 Questions and Answers About Muslim Americans.* Canton, MI: Read the Spirit Books, 2014.

Websites

Arab American Institute

http://www.aaiusa.org
This educational site contains links to news stories, policy initiatives, and events where you can help fight anti-Muslim actions.

Bridge Initiative at Georgetown University

http://bridge.georgetown.edu
The Jesuit university is conducting a research project which it says connects the academic study of Islamophobia with the public square.

Council on American-Islamic Relations (CAIR)

http://www.cair.com
Everything from news stories to legislative initiatives to an explanation of Islam can be found at this comprehensive site.

Shoulder-to-Shoulder Campaign

http://www.shouldertoshouldercampaign.org
An interfaith group tries to end anti-Muslim feelings by supporting local and regional efforts.

Southern Poverty Law Center Hate Map

https://www.splcenter.org/hate-map
View the location of 892 hate groups, as laid out by the Southern Poverty Law Center.

Stand Against Bigotry Campaign

https://standagainstbigotry.com
The People for the American Way fight Islamophobia by exposing anti-Muslim extremism.

Videos

"Muslim Burr Ridge Teen's Life in America"

https://www.youtube.com/watch?v=TvbjAP9Mxgo
The *Chicago Tribune* interviews a Muslim teenager about her faith and her life in the United States.

"PBS America at a Crossroads: The Muslim Americans"

https://www.youtube.com/watch?v=WQ0dJ8yuF78
This program focuses on the experiences of the diverse groups of Muslims in the United States after 9/11, and contrasts life for Muslims in the US to Muslims in Britain and Europe.

Books

Ernst, Carl W., ed. *Islamophobia in America: The Anatomy of Intolerance.* New York: Palgrave Macmillan, 2013.

GhaneaBassiri, Kambiz. *A History of Islam in America.* New York: Cambridge University Press, 2010.

Green, Todd H. *The Fear of Islam: An Introduction to Islamophobia in the West.* Minneapolis, MN: Fortress Press, 2015.

Kumar, Deepa. *Islamophobia and the Politics of Empire.* Chicago: Haymarket Books, 2012.

McCloud, Aminah Beverly, Scott W. Hibbard, and Laith Saud, eds. *An Introduction to Islam in the 21st Century.* West Sussex, UK: Wiley-Blackwell, 2013.

Online Articles

Ali, Wajahat, Eli Clifton, Matthew Duss, Lee Fang, Scott Keyes, and Faiz Shakir. *Fear, Inc.: The Roots of the Islamophobia Network in America.* Center For American Progress, August 26, 2011. https://www.americanprogress.org/issues/religion/report/2011/08/26/10165/fear-inc.

American Civil Liberties Union. "Factsheet: The NYPD Muslim Surveillance Program." ACLU.org. Accessed August 1, 2016. https://www.aclu.org/factsheet-nypd-muslim-surveillance-program.

——— . "Surveillance Under The Patriot Act." ACLU.org. Accessed August 1, 2016. https://www.aclu.org/infographic/surveillance-under-patriot-act.

Berenstein, Erica, Nick Corasaniti, and Ashley Parker. "Unfiltered Voices from Donald Trump's Crowds." *New York Times,* August 3, 2016. http://www.nytimes.com/video/us/politics/100000004533191/unfiltered-voices-from-donald-trumps-crowds.html.

Blumberg, Antonia. "A Guide to Gun Stores and Ranges Declaring 'Muslim-Free' Zones." *Huffington Post,* August 14, 2015. http://www.huffingtonpost.com/entry/gun-stores-muslim-free-zones_us_55ce4e52e4b07addcb430539.

Brumfield, Ben. "All Schools Shut Down in Augusta County, Virginia, Over Islam Homework." CNN.com, December 19, 2015. http://www.cnn.com/2015/12/18/us/virginia-school-shut-islam-homework/index.html?sr=twCNN121815virginia-school-shut-islam-homework0156PMVODtopLink&linkId=19696813.

Carrega-Woodby, Christina. "Four Brooklyn Men Claim They Were Kicked Off Flight for Looking Too Muslim in Lawsuit." *New York Daily News,* January 18, 2016. http://www.nydailynews.com/new-york/lawsuit-claims-flight-ejected-men-muslim-article-1.2499843.

Council on American-Islamic Relations. "CAIR Launches Satirical 'ISLAMOPHOBIN' Public Awareness Campaign to Challenge Anti-Muslim Bigotry." cair.com, June 25, 2016. https://www.cair.com/press-center/press-releases/13554-cair-launches-satirical-islamophobin-public-awareness-campaign-to-challenge-anti-muslim-bigotry.html.

Dowd, Maureen. "Trump's Thunderbolts." *New York Times,* July 29, 2016. http://www.nytimes.com/2016/07/30/opinion/trumps-thunderbolts.html.

Fahrenthold, David A., and Michelle Boorstein. "Rep. Peter King's Muslim Hearings: A Key Moment in Angry Conversation."

Washington Post, March 9, 2011. http://www.
washingtonpost.com/wp-dyn/content/article/2011/03/09/
AR2011030902061.html?sid=ST2011031002070.

"Full Text: Khizr Khan's Speech to the 2016 Democratic National
Convention." ABC News, August 1, 2016. http://abcnews.
go.com/Politics/full-text-khizr-khans-speech-2016-democratic-
national/story?id=41043609.

Geller, Pamela. "Monster Mosque Pushes Ahead in Shadow of World
Trade Center Islamic Death and Destruction." *Atlas Shrugs*, May
6, 2010. http://pamelageller.com/2010/05/monster-mosque-
pushes-ahead-in-shadow-of-world-trade-center-islamic-death-and-
destruction.html.

Goldman, Adam, and Matt Apuzzo. "Informant: NYPD Paid Me to
Bait Muslims." Associated Press, October 23, 2012. http://www.
ap.org/Content/AP-In-The-News/2012/Informant-NYPD-paid-me-
to-bait-Muslims.

Green, Emma. "The Fear of Islam in Tennessee Public Schools."
Atlantic, December 16, 2015. http://www.theatlantic.com/
education/archive/2015/12/fear-islam-tennessee-public-
schools/420441.

H., Lamya. "A Personal History of Islamophobia in
America." *Vox*, January 15, 2016. http://www.vox.
com/2016/1/15/10767904/islamophobia-immigrant-america.

Harvard, Sarah. "Mohamed Ahmed Radwan Kicked Off Plane After
Flight Attendant Said 'You Will Be Watched.'" *Mic*, July 21,
2016. https://mic.com/articles/149420/mohamed-ahmed-
radwan-kicked-off-plane-after-flight-attendant-said-you-will-be-
watched#.1vOMEBuqO.

"Highlights of AP's Pulitzer Prize–Winning Probe into NYPD Intelligence Operations." Associated Press. Accessed August 1, 2016. http://www.ap.org/media-center/nypd/investigation.

"How Trump's Plan to Ban Muslims Has Evolved Over Time." Associated Press, June 28, 2016. http://fortune. com/2016/06/28/donald-trump-muslim-ban.

Kaplan, Rebecca. "Ted Cruz: 'No Meaningful Risk' of Christian Terror," CBS News, November 16, 2015. http://www.cbsnews. com/news/paris-attacks-ted-cruz-no-meaningful-risk-of-christian-terror.

Kessler, Glen. "Trump's Outrageous Claim That 'Thousands' of New Jersey Muslims Celebrated the 9/11 Attacks." *Washington Post*, November 22, 2015. https://www.washingtonpost.com/news/ fact-checker/wp/2015/11/22/donald-trumps-outrageous-claim-that-thousands-of-new-jersey-muslims-celebrated-the-911-attacks.

Kittel, Olivia. "Right-Wing Media's Worst Islamophobic Rhetoric." Media Matters, January 11, 2015. http://mediamatters.org/ research/2015/01/11/right-wing-medias-worst-islamophobic-rhetoric/202087.

Najafizada, Enayat, and Rod Nordland. "Afghans Avenge Florida Koran Burning, Killing 12." *New York Times*, April 1, 2011. http://www.nytimes.com/2011/04/02/world/ asia/02afghanistan.html?pagewanted=1.

Prager, Dennis. "America, Not Keith Ellison, Decides What Book a Congressman Takes His Oath On," Townhall.com, November 28, 2006. http://townhall.com/columnists/ dennisprager/2006/11/28/america,_not_keith_ellison,_ decides_what_book_a_congressman_takes_his_oath_on.

Silber, Mitchell D., and Arvin Bhatt. "Radicalization in the West: The Homegrown Threat." NYPD Intelligence Division, August 2007. https://www.brennancenter.org/sites/default/files/legacy/Justice/20070816.NYPD.Radicalization.in.the.West.pdf.

Southern Poverty Law Center. "Anti-Muslim Incidents Since Sept. 11, 2001." splcenter.org. Accessed August 1, 2016. https://www.splcenter.org/news/2011/03/29/anti-muslim-incidents-sept-11-2001.

Steinback, Robert. "The Anti-Muslim Inner Circle." splcenter.org, June 17, 2011. https://www.splcenter.org/fighting-hate/intelligence-report/2011/anti-muslim-inner-circle.

———. "Jihad Against Islam." splcenter.org, June 17, 2011. https://www.splcenter.org/fighting-hate/intelligence-report/2011/jihad-against-islam.

Stone, Shomari. "Virginia Woman Says She Was Fired for Wearing Hijab." nbcwashington.com, August 4, 2016. http://www.nbcwashington.com/news/local/Virginia-Woman-Says-She-Was-Fired-for-Wearing-Hijab-389134252.html.

Williams, Timothy. "The Hated and the Hater, Both Touched By Crime," New York Times, July 18, 2011. http://www.nytimes.com/2011/07/19/us/19questions.html?_r=0.

"Zelenik Issues Statement on Proposed Islamic Center." Murfreesboro Post, June 24, 2010. http://www.murfreesboropost.com/zelenik-issues-statement-on-proposed-islamic-center-cms-23606.

INDEX

violence, 8–9, 11, 29–30, 30, 32, 34, 57–61, 112
workplace discrimination, 84–85
isolationism, 12

Jews, 6, 11–12, 15, 18–21, 19, 29, 108, 112–113
jihad, 43, 45–46, 63, 65–66, 68, 70, 95, 102, 107, 110

Khan, Khizr and Ghazala, 110–113, 111
Ku Klux Klan, 17–18, 103

Maher, Bill, 76
monolithic, 6
mosque crawlers, 62–63
mujahideen, 43, 45

nativism, 12, 99–100
NYPD, 61–66

Obama, Barack, 37, 51–52, 73, 106–107
Oklahoma City bombing, 32–35
othering, 6, 12, 52, 77

Paris attacks (2015), 98, 101–102, 104, 106
Park51, 67–69, 71, 77, 86, 93
pogrom, 18
power vacuum, 44, 54

proxy war, 43
Pulse nightclub shooting, 105, 106

rakers, 61–62
refugees, 9, 18, 23, 44, 101–102, 106–107
Robertson, Pat, 76–77

Salafi, 65
San Bernardino shooting, 103, 105, 107
September 11 attacks, 5–7, 31, 35, 36, 37–42, 39, 48, 51, 57–61, 67, 69, 71–72, 74, 77–79, 93, 95–96, 101, 105–106
shahada, 82
sharia, 70, 74, 77, 89, 95
Sikhs, 8, 11, 57, 59, 79–80

think tank, 6, 70
Trump, Donald, 9, 90–91 99, 101, 106–109, 111–112

white nationalism, 99
World Trade Center bombing (1993), 31–32

xenophobia, 9, 14, 99

zakat, 95

ABOUT THE AUTHOR

Alison Morretta holds a Bachelor of Arts in English and Creative Writing from Kenyon College in Gambier, Ohio, where she studied literature and American history. She has written many nonfiction titles for middle and high school students on subjects such as the abolitionist movement, American literature, and internet safety. She lives in New York City with her loving husband, Bart, and their rambunctious Corgi, Cassidy.